Undaunted Ursula Franklin

# Undaunted Ursula Franklin
## Activist, Educator, Scientist

Monica Franklin
& Erin Della Mattia

Second Story Press

Library and Archives Canada Cataloguing in Publication

Title: Undaunted Ursula Franklin : activist, educator, scientist / Monica Franklin & Erin Della Mattia.
Names: Franklin, Monica, author. | Della Mattia, Erin, author.
Identifiers: Canadiana (print) 20240393996 | Canadiana (ebook) 20240394399 | ISBN 9781772603897 (softcover) | ISBN 9781772603996 (EPUB)
Subjects: LCSH: Franklin, Ursula M., 1921-2016—Juvenile literature. | LCSH: Women political activists—Canada—Biography—Juvenile literature. | LCSH: Political activists—Canada—Biography—Juvenile literature. | LCSH: Women pacifists—Canada—Biography—Juvenile literature. | LCSH: Pacifists—Canada—Biography—Juvenile literature. | LCSH: Women scientists—Canada—Biography—Juvenile literature. | LCSH: Scientists—Canada—Biography—Juvenile literature. | LCSH: Women college teachers—Canada—Biography—Juvenile literature. | LCSH: College teachers—Canada—Biography—Juvenile literature. | LCGFT: Biographies.
Classification: LCC HQ1455.F73 F73 2024 | DDC 305.4092—dc23

Copyright © 2024 Monica Franklin and Erin Della Mattia
Edited by Kathryn Cole
Cover illustration by Hannah McAvoy (www.hannahmcavoy.com)
Book design by Laura Atherton
Printed and bound in Canada

*Second Story Press gratefully acknowledges the support of the Ontario Arts Council and the Canada Council for the Arts for our publishing program. We acknowledge the financial support of the Government of Canada through the Canada Book Fund.*

Second Story Press expressly prohibits the use of *Undaunted Ursula Franklin* in connection with the development of any software program, including, without limitation, training a machine learning or generative artificial intelligence (AI) system.

Published by
SECOND STORY PRESS
20 Maud Street, Suite 401
Toronto, ON M5V 2M5
www.secondstorypress.ca

*To my mother: whose courage, strength, and love continue to guide me.*

—**MF**

*For the next generation of feminist scientists.*

—**EDM**

# Foreword

Have you ever seen a street or a school with a person's name and wondered why it was named after them? Maybe it's someone you've never heard of. What did they do? Were they famous? Now, imagine if that person was your mother. This is the story of Ursula Franklin—a Canadian scientist, activist, and feminist—as told through the eyes of her daughter, Monica.

Monica and Martin Franklin beneath the street sign for Ursula Franklin Street in Toronto.

# Part I

Life in Germany

# Chapter 1

# Ursula the Student

Applause echoes cheerfully through the grand concert hall. With instruments in hand, members of the Berlin Philharmonic Orchestra rise and bow. Ursula stands too, clapping so hard that her hands tingle when she stops. She and her parents follow the crowd out of the hall and into the vast, golden lobby. She's wearing one of her best dresses; the navy blue one with small pink flowers printed on it. Her shiny black shoes click as she walks across the marble floor and out through the doors. Though the inside of the concert hall was dim, outside it is bright and sunny. People on the street bustle to cafés and shops.

    Ursula's parents debate whether to go home to prepare dinner, or if they should go to a park and enjoy the rest of the day. Ursula pleads for the park, and laughing, they agree. But as the family strolls forward, a chilly breeze interrupts them. Everyone has become strangely quiet, their gazes shifting down the street to where a group of teenage boys are marching toward the concert hall. They're all dressed the same: brown shorts, beige shirts, brown ties, and red bands with the Nazi symbol on them. All the warmth Ursula felt from the concert disappears, replaced by unease and uncertainty. She holds her breath until the boys move past. Without a word, her family turns around and walks home.

Ursula doesn't know it yet, but she has reason to be afraid. Her future has some staggering roadblocks in store for her.

My mother, Ursula Maria Martius, was born on September 16, 1921, in Munich, Germany. When she was very young, her parents moved to the capital city of Berlin, where she spent most of her childhood. Because her parents loved art and history, their old house was filled with artworks and artifacts. Ursula's father, Albrecht, was an archaeologist, and her mother, Ilse, was an art historian. It's no wonder Ursula grew up loving art and history too.

Even when her parents were busy with their work, Ursula was free to wander around the living room, looking at all the artifacts. As long as she was careful, she was allowed to touch anything she wanted. She would open the display cabinet and

In 1910, Ursula's father had traveled to Africa with the well-known German adventurer, Leo Frobenius, on his famous expedition to the Kingdom of Benin (now part of Nigeria). He found ancient objects created by the Yoruba people, one of Africa's oldest civilizations. At the time, Europeans didn't know much about African cultures. Some even thought they were inferior. Ursula learned from her father that African cultures weren't inferior, just unfamiliar. That made her even more curious.

lift out different things to examine. A large bronze figure of an antelope was one of her favorites. It was heavy in her hands as she stroked the smooth metal and traced the designs etched on its surface. Her father had brought back the antelope from one of his trips to Africa long before she was born. He had explained that the Yoruba metal workers created such figures by pouring hot liquid metal into molds.

"But *who* made the molds?" she had asked. "And *how* did they make them?"

Her father could only smile and admit he didn't know.

Ursula gently put the antelope back on the display shelf and then chose another of her favorite pieces; a bowl made from a dried gourd. The bowl was very light. Fancy designs of black triangles and squares marched across its surface. Looking closely, Ursula noticed that the bowl didn't look like it had been used for cooking. Maybe someone had used it to hold fruit or nuts or sweets? She pictured a woman filling the bowl with treats for visitors. But then those same questions interrupted her imaginings: *Who* made the bowl? And *how*? Ursula didn't want to *imagine*—she wanted to *know*.

> In the 1920s it was quite unusual for women to work outside the home as historians, scientists, doctors, or businesspeople. Most of Ursula's relatives, on both sides of her family, had university educations and professional jobs. That included the women, like Ilse and her two sisters. For Ursula, it meant she had a lot of role models. She learned early on that women could do anything they wanted. They could study and work even in male-dominated fields such as science and math.

Pleased with how eager their only child was to learn, my grandparents took Ursula to Berlin's museums and art galleries. On special occasions, the family would dress up in their nicest clothes to attend concerts by the Berlin Philharmonic Orchestra. The concert hall itself was a spectacle with huge glass chandeliers hanging from the ornate ceiling.

Ursula as a young girl.

> Hitler and the Nazis hated Jews. They believed there was a superior German "Aryan" race and that all non-Aryans—particularly Jews, but also Black, disabled, Romani, and LGBTQ+ people—were inferior and "impure." Hitler created laws that discriminated against Jews. Storekeepers could refuse to sell them food, and doctors could refuse to treat them. The Nazis controlled where Jewish people could live, work, study, shop, when they could ride public transit, and even if they could own pets.

Ursula also loved the zoo. The Berlin Zoological Garden was huge! It housed more than twenty thousand animals and just as many plants. Every time she went to the zoo, Mom saw something she hadn't even heard of before.

In the all-girls' public school that Ursula attended, she was just as eager to learn. Most of the girls chatted together about things they had done on the weekends, but Ursula preferred to focus on her schoolwork. She enjoyed science and loved puzzles—putting things together, taking them apart, and discovering how they worked. She wanted to understand how small parts of things play a role in creating something bigger. Like how the small filament in a lightbulb produces light, or how pulleys and cables can lift an elevator full of people.

My mother excelled at school, and she planned to continue her studies at university. But that wasn't going to be as straightforward as it might have been. A dark shadow of fear and hate soon spread across her city, her country, and out into the world, blotting out the happiness and artistic spirit she had known all her life.

Ursula had just started high school when Adolf Hitler came to power in 1933. Berlin became the center of his Nazi regime. Ursula tried to keep focused on her studies, but it was very hard to ignore what was happening around her.

In August 1936, the Summer Olympic Games were held in Berlin. My mother was almost sixteen by then. She told me that she, like all schoolchildren in Berlin, was required to attend, because the Olympics were to be a showcase for the Nazis.

Jesse Owens did not win one gold medal at the Berlin Olympics—he won *four*, making him the most successful athlete there at just twenty-two years old!

Berlin's Olympic Stadium was packed with over one hundred thousand noisy, excited people. Hitler was determined that these games would prove the "pure Aryan race" was superior to all others, and that his racist beliefs were popular. By doing so, his goal to rid Germany of Jews and people who were "different" would be easier to achieve. His dreadful hatred would spread... that is if the German team lived up to his expectations. Sitting in the audience, Ursula remembered her father's lesson from so long ago. Different people and cultures were not inferior or dangerous. They were simply unfamiliar.

Ursula scanned the athletes gathering in the stadium. She wanted to catch a glimpse of Jesse Owens, the Black American track star who had a chance to win gold here. Secretly she hoped he would. That would show Hitler with all his big talk about the white Aryan race!

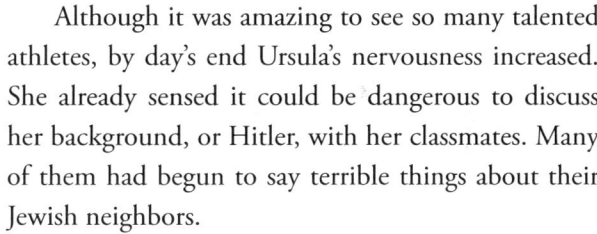

Hitler's campaign against the Jews became more violent over the years. On one particular night in November 1938, Hitler ordered his Nazi military troops and supporters to steal from and destroy Jewish homes and businesses across Germany and Austria. This night became known as *Kristallnacht*, or the Night of Broken Glass. Jewish families hid in their homes as best they could, terrified that they would be targeted next. The troops also arrested over thirty thousand Jewish men and imprisoned them in concentration camps. Concentration camps are prisons that powerful people like Hitler use to control or punish those whom they want to destroy.

Suddenly, a hush fell over the crowd, and everyone rose to their feet. Ursula squinted into the distance and watched Adolf Hitler, surrounded by his officials, walk into his private viewing box. Many in the audience saluted him. Ursula shivered.

Although it was amazing to see so many talented athletes, by day's end Ursula's nervousness increased. She already sensed it could be dangerous to discuss her background, or Hitler, with her classmates. Many of them had begun to say terrible things about their Jewish neighbors.

Everything felt so wrong now. The very next day, Ursula discovered that the nearby bakery she had gone to all her life had closed down. Ilse had sent her to buy a loaf of rye bread, but when she arrived, she found the door locked and the shop dark and empty. She heard

Ilse Martius

Ursula the Student     5

neighbors whispering about how the Jewish owners had fled during the night.

As time passed, my mother noticed that more and more people were disappearing. One day her next-door neighbors were there, and the next, they were gone. Some of her classmates vanished as the Nazis forced Jewish children out of school and their parents out of work. Desks would stand empty, but only for a day or two. The teacher would quickly change the seating plan and move another student into that vacant spot, hoping no one would notice their classmate's absence. Ursula sometimes wondered how many more students would have to leave school. How many more dreams would come to an end.

At first, Ursula's parents believed their family wouldn't be affected by the Nazis. They only seemed to be going after people who were Jewish on both sides of the family and who practiced their faith. Although Ilse was born Jewish, she had not been raised in a religious household. She had never gone to a synagogue and did not know Jewish customs, or the Yiddish language. Plus, Albrecht came from a prominent Protestant family. He thought that alone would keep them all safe. With conditions growing more complicated by the day, it was advisable for Ursula not to mention her mother's background. She continued to go to school and her parents worked, as if everything was normal. But everything was far from normal.

One day the family sat down together at the dinner table to come up with a plan for Ursula to attend university in a safer country, far away from Germany. They didn't talk about it often—not until they really had to. But for a short time at least, having a plan was a small comfort.

Then the Nazis changed their focus. They had already arrested

Albrecht Martius's passport.

**6** Undaunted Ursula Franklin

and imprisoned almost everyone who had Jewish blood on both sides of their families. Many more Jews, fearing the worst, had left the country. So, the Nazis began to target those who had any Jewish ancestry at all. They went to people's workplaces and barged into their homes, arresting anyone they suspected of being part Jewish. Ursula's mother became a target. And since she was half Jewish, Ursula was a target too.

Ilse quickly realized the danger she and her family were facing. She was afraid they would be arrested and wanted them all to leave the country as soon as possible. But Albrecht couldn't believe things would get that bad. He argued that his family had a long and distinguished history in Germany. They had been important members of the government, universities, and the church. Albrecht himself had fought in the First World War and had received medals for his bravery. He was sure they would be safe.

Until Ursula's father came home one afternoon, took off his hat, sat down at the dinner table, and sadly announced that he had been forced to leave his engineering job. Why? He was married to a Jew. He finally agreed that the time had come for the three of them to leave Germany…if they could.

Albrecht thought it was important to let his family know of their plans. He visited his brother's home, hopeful of their support. But instead, his brother revealed something that shocked Albrecht: his relatives didn't want anything to do with it. They believed what the Nazis had said: that Albrecht had been "tainted" by his marriage to Ilse, a woman with Jewish ancestry. It made all three of them—Ursula and her parents—Jewish. Albrecht's family didn't want to be seen talking to or supporting Jews.

Not long ago, when my brother and I were looking through some of our mother's mementos, Martin discovered a photo. In it, Hitler was kneeling to talk to four young boys wearing traditional German outfits. At the bottom of the photo, our mother had written "Der Fuhrer [Hitler] with my cousins."

We were stunned. Members of Albrecht's own family had supported Hitler and what he stood for! Where had this picture come from? And why had our

Hitler with four young boys wearing traditional German outfits. At the bottom of the photo, Ursula has written, "Der Fuhrer [Hitler] with my cousins." These are Ursula's cousins on her father's side.

mother kept it all these years? It must have been important to her. But why would she keep a photo of Hitler, when his beliefs caused so much pain, suffering, and disruption?

Ursula didn't like to talk about her early years—for many Holocaust survivors, it's just too difficult. Seeing this photo of her cousins with Hitler made my brother and me realize how little we knew about our mom's life before she came to Canada. It explained some things too.

"This might be why Mother didn't talk much about her father's side of the family," Martin said to me.

Ursula must have been devastated that her relatives did not support Albrecht during this time. If she had been close to these cousins as a child, this betrayal would have been particularly painful. Any good memories of them were poisoned by the events leading up to the Second World War.

With or without the support of Albrecht's family, our grandparents were determined to get their daughter out of Germany. If they couldn't escape too, at least she would be safe. But safety wouldn't come easily. Many countries had become infected by Hitler's beliefs, and they did not want Jews coming to live there. Still, Ursula and her parents tried to find a way to leave Germany. Ursula diligently applied for scholarships to universities throughout Europe. At last, she was successful. She won a scholarship to study in England!

The college sent her a letter requesting her to obtain a student visa, which would give her permission to go to school there. But there was a problem. She had to be eighteen years or older to obtain a student visa. Ursula filled out the forms and got all the paperwork ready to submit to the British government on September 16, the day she turned eighteen. But on September 1, 1939, just *fifteen* days before her birthday, Germany invaded Poland. Two days later, England declared war on Germany. The Second World War had begun. It was impossible for Ursula to leave the country.

If my mother had been born two or three weeks earlier, what a different life she might have led. She might have escaped the horrors of war. Instead, she was trapped.

# Chapter 2

# Ursula the Laborer

Snow crunches under the guard's boots as he paces back and forth. Ursula knows without looking that he holds a gun. In front of her is a gaping hole where the brick wall of a factory used to be. It has been blasted apart by a bomb, and the Nazis want it repaired. They'll turn the building into an ammunitions factory to make bullets. After the wall is finished, Ursula will have to go up the ladder to repair the roof. That's the worst—the cold on her bare legs. Ursula rubs her hands together and blows on her fingers to bring the feeling back into them. Prisoners aren't allowed gloves. Suddenly, the guard stops right behind her. She stiffens, then takes a deep breath and gets back to work. The snow starts to fall again.

With the beginning of the war, all of Berlin was tense. Soldiers were everywhere: on the streets and sidewalks, inside stores and public buildings. Ursula couldn't go anywhere without feeling their cold stares. Venturing outside was difficult. Many roads leading out of the city were closed and others were blocked. People had to identify themselves to pass through checkpoints that the Nazis had set up. They were looking for Jews, especially Jews trying to escape. Ursula hated the checkpoints. She had to be ready to explain where she was going, how long she would stay, and when she would be returning home. She always carried identification documents with her, showing who she was and where she lived. Sometimes the lineups in front of her were long, and they moved slowly if people didn't have all their papers ready and in order. The officials looked for any excuse to refuse people entry or to haul them away altogether.

At home, Ursula could hear the fighting in the streets or bombers overhead. Because Berlin was the center of Nazi activity, it was a target for the Allied (English, French, and Soviet) forces. The first bombs dropped on Berlin in August 1940, just as Ursula was preparing to start university in her home country. The city would be struck hundreds of times

Ursula's childhood home in Berlin.

over the course of the war. Whenever the warning sirens wailed, Ursula and her parents turned off all the lights so their home wouldn't be visible from the sky. Then they sheltered in the cellar, waiting until it was safe to come out. If the siren sounded when Ursula was outside, she and everyone else on the street would run to shelter in basements and underground subway stations. Once the bombing had stopped, Ursula would rush back home to make sure her parents were safe, and their house was still standing.

To attend classes, Ursula had to walk through streets lined with rubble and bombed buildings, carefully avoiding walls that could fall over. Glass crunched under her feet as she passed by people digging through the wreckage of their homes and businesses. Every day, she wondered if she would even make it to class. If she did, would the teacher be there? Would there be enough of her fellow students for the lecture to be taught? And every minute during class, she listened for fighting and bombs outside. It was difficult to concentrate on her studies, but Ursula knew that she wouldn't be any safer at home. She wouldn't be safe anywhere in Germany, now that bombs were falling, and Nazi soldiers had widened their search for anyone with any Jewish heritage.

As an adult, my mother always had incredible focus and the ability to block out all distractions around her. When she was reading, she wouldn't hear my brother and me talking, even if we were standing right beside her. We'd answer the phone or the door because she wouldn't have heard the ring! I think she probably learned to focus like that during the war, when the relentless barrage of bombs was as commonplace as an ambulance siren or honking horn. If she could learn to ignore that—to sleep or to study—she could ignore anything.

Even though she faced discrimination and risked being forced out of her education, Ursula persevered with her studies. She attended the University of Berlin where she studied math and chemistry, with a special focus on physics. She was still curious about how things are made and how the different parts fit together to make something move, or heat up, or run. Ursula also liked that physics and math were based in facts. Facts were one thing the Nazis could not change.

Because she was a "half-Jew," Ursula needed special permission to attend her classes. Every month, she had to ask the university to renew her "guest student" permit. How unwelcome she must have felt, but knowing my mom, I'm sure this also strengthened her determination. She would prove to them how much she deserved to be there.

Alongside the dangers from bombs and soldiers outside the school, there were dangers inside the university too. Many of Ursula's professors and fellow students supported the Nazis. Even those who *didn't* support them had to pretend to, or risk losing their jobs. Students were expected to report anyone who helped Jews or didn't support Hitler's evil plan. The Nazis had already forced all those who were fully Jewish out of the university: professors, staff, and students. As Ursula noticed teachers and fellow students disappear around her, she clung to the hope that some had escaped the country or gone into hiding. Despite her hopes, she knew many had been arrested and imprisoned in concentration camps. She was also aware that the same thing could happen to her. Ursula wondered how much longer she would be able to go to university. She was only allowed to take classes because she had a guest student permit. That could change at any time. And then what?

It wasn't long before she found out. In January 1942, Ursula was forced to leave the university. Because my mother never spoke of it, I wonder how it happened. Perhaps she was quietly given a letter saying that her permit to study was canceled and she was no longer welcome. But it could have been more dramatic. Soldiers might have stopped her at the classroom door, refusing to let her enter. If that was the case, did her fellow students react, or did they just watch silently from their seats?

Mother kept diaries and journals throughout her life. Her wartime ones are in her collection at the University of Toronto Archives. I picture her clenching the pen and struggling to find the words to describe everything happening around her. I know she was humiliated and angry at being expelled. She had finished most of her courses and was an excellent student, but she was not allowed to take her final exams and graduate. Everything she had worked for seemed to be for nothing.

But then things got much worse. Shortly after she was expelled, Ursula and her mother were walking on the street when they were arrested by the Nazis' secret police force. They were immediately separated. Ursula was taken to a forced labor camp in Berlin, the name of which she never said. She had no idea where her mother was.

Albrecht and Ursula.

Nor did she know anything about her father's fate. Was he safe at home, or had he been arrested too? She desperately hoped he had not been taken but feared he had. The whole time Ursula was in the labor camp, she didn't know whether her parents were dead or alive. Communication was impossible. At just twenty years of age, my mother was suddenly torn from her home, her parents—her entire life.

Ursula could at least find comfort in one thing. Fearing the worst, she and her parents had made a plan. If any or all of them were taken by the Nazis and survived, they would meet at the family house in Berlin. That hope to reunite with her family sustained Ursula for the next eighteen months.

Work in the forced labor camp was backbreaking, and the conditions were terrible. Often there wasn't enough food, clothing, shelter, or medical care. For some Jews, labor was their only hope of surviving the war. If they had skills that were useful to the Nazis, they could avoid being sent to a death camp. Ursula did have a useful skill—science. So she was put to work in a factory that made radio and telegraph communication equipment. It was not just difficult physical work. It must have been very difficult emotionally too. Mom and the other prisoners were being forced to help the very people who wanted them dead.

Ursula also repaired bombed buildings. She had to work outdoors in all kinds of weather and without proper clothing or equipment. She got frostbite from the cold. For the rest of her life, my mother had poor circulation in her legs, feet, and hands. Once she was chilled, it took her a long time to warm up. Returning home after a short winter walk, Martin and I would throw off our coats and hats and rush to the kitchen for something to eat. We'd come back to find Mom in the front room, holding her frozen, white fingers up to the heater, or in the bathroom, running warm water over them.

Ursula was released from the forced labor camp after eighteen months. As she and her parents had planned, she made her way to the family house in northern Berlin. Miraculously, it was still standing. Soldiers had used it for shelter. It had been looted and all their furniture and belongings taken, but the house was empty

Situated in Lower Saxony, Bergen-Belsen was established in 1940 as a prisoner-of-war camp. Shortly after, however, it was used as a concentration/death camp for Jews and others persecuted by the Nazis. Between 1940 and 1945, more than 70,000 people perished in Bergen-Belsen alone.

of people. Somehow, Ursula survived on her own, waiting for her parents to join her as they had planned, and terrified that they wouldn't.

Her mother arrived home next: she had been sent to a concentration camp in Berlin. It took almost two more years for her father to be released: he had been arrested and taken to a concentration camp in Saxony, in the eastern part of Germany. He was sixty-one years old. Their reunion must have been incredibly emotional. Ursula's parents were deeply affected by their experiences in the camps. They had physical scars which would eventually heal, but the emotional ones would last forever.

◆

Some Holocaust survivors share their experiences of the war. They write books, create movies and art, and give lectures to help people understand what they went through. By offering a record of what happened, they hope they can help prevent such an atrocity from ever happening again.

My mother was a private person. She spent her life focusing on the present and the future, not the past. Sometimes when Ursula was interviewed, she was asked about the war. Her answers were usually brief. In one interview, when asked how she survived, my mom answered with only one word: "Painfully." She was asked by many people over the years if they could write her life story. She always refused, saying they could not possibly understand what she had gone through.

Growing up, Martin and I knew the war was horrible and had completely changed our mother's life. But back then I didn't fully understand what that meant. Mom preferred to focus on the "here and now," sharing her enthusiasm for art and culture with my brother and me. She often took us to the Royal Ontario Museum (ROM) in Toronto, where we spent hours looking at ancient objects. Mother was particularly fond of the African galleries, probably because they reminded her of her father.

But the past? That was another thing. Even if I'd asked more questions, I doubt Mom would have answered them. She likely thought Martin and I were too young to understand. And she may have been right. Her world had been full of horrors, destruction, and heartbreak; experiences that would have been unimaginable to us then.

It was only after Mother's death that my brother and I began to piece things together. Among the many boxes she left behind was one with our grandfather Albrecht's name on it in Mom's handwriting. When I went through it, I found a document. It showed that Albrecht had received monthly compensation from the German government for his injuries and because the family house had been used by the military while he, Ilse, and Ursula were imprisoned. I learned from Erika, a close friend of Mother's, that Ursula's uncle was killed in the fighting. One of her aunts also died in Theresienstadt, a notorious concentration camp. Erika couldn't tell me any more—Ursula never shared their names, or where her uncle was killed.

I wish I had known sooner. It makes me sad that Mom was not able to tell me herself. I wonder who my great-aunt and great-uncle were, what they were like, and if Ursula had been close to them before the war. I wonder about Ursula's story. How did she find her way home after leaving the labor camp? Did she escape, or was she released? Did she have food? Did anyone help her, or was she completely alone? So many questions make me wonder about all the other families who had similar stories. Eleven million people were killed during the Holocaust, six million of them had Jewish ancestry, like Ursula.

I can understand now why these experiences were too difficult to talk about. And I can definitely see how they shaped my mother's life in the years to come.

# Chapter 3

# Ursula the Survivor

Ursula sits at her bedroom window, watching her father work in their garden. With food so scarce, she and her family need this garden to survive. As her father stoops to water vegetables, two soldiers appear at the fence. The sun glints off their pistols. The men yell something at Albrecht and then start toward the door. Ursula rushes out of her room, up the ladder, and into the attic to hide. She shuts the trapdoor, making sure it's firmly bolted from the inside. The attic is dark, except for a few pale slits of light leaking in where bombs have shaken the rooftiles loose. Ursula's heart thumps so loudly she thinks the soldiers might hear it. Sounds of banging and smashing come from the kitchen below—the soldiers searching through drawers and cupboards for anything valuable. Terrified, Ursula huddles silently in the darkness of a corner...and waits.

The final days of the war were horrific for Ursula and her family. Tanks and soldiers mobbed the streets of Berlin, and bombers fractured the air day and night. Fortunate to still have their house, Ursula and her parents often slept—or at least tried to sleep—fully clothed in the cellar, ready for anything. Even if they managed to rest, the days were living nightmares. Much of the city had been reduced to rubble. The Allied forces hadn't only bombed military targets. They had also destroyed monuments, churches, schools, and homes. Gone were the galleries and parks that Ursula had loved as a child. In their place were ruins and tree stumps. The population of Berlin was half of what it had been. Many citizens had been killed or imprisoned or had fled the country. Those whose homes had been destroyed, had to find shelter in what churches were still standing, abandoned buildings, or underground subway stations.

The whole country was under martial law, which meant the military was in charge. No one could leave their property. It was almost impossible to get around anyway. There was no gas for cars and the transit system had shut down. The only thing people could do was wait and hope for the fighting to end.

Ursula and her parents, quite understandably, were afraid of Nazi soldiers. But as the days dragged on, different uniforms began to appear outside their windows. It was hard to know if they were Soviet, French, British, or American. Were these military men going to liberate their city, or would the fighting just go on and on? Soldiers often broke into people's homes to steal food, alcohol, or valuables. It was also risky to keep a diary—the Nazis did not want a record of all the terrible things they had done. But Ursula bravely recorded her family's experiences during the last days of the war.

Ursula's diaries are among all the other documents and audio recordings she put in her collection at the University of Toronto Archives—more than 150 boxes! Martin and I had a few of the pages of her diary from this time translated. Ursula wrote that her parents kept all the curtains drawn, doors locked, and lights off. In her entry for April 27, 1945, she wrote about soldiers forcing their way into her home and that they didn't find much: "We had long ago taken off jewelry and watches and hidden them." The next day, she tells how soldiers broke down the garden gate and came into the house. She "slips into her attic hiding place" but she could hear the soldiers in the living room below. She writes that she doesn't hear

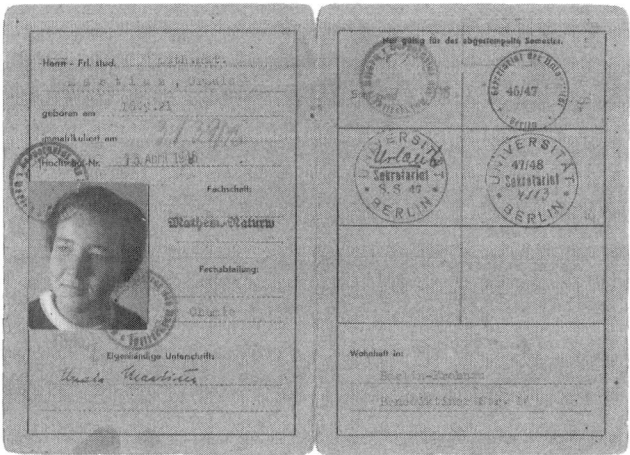

Ursula's student identification document (ID). Each stamp marks a different school semester.

"too much ransacking of drawers…too much stealing, but it requires all of Father's and Mother's diplomacy to prevent worse." Usually, if soldiers came anywhere near their house, Ursula hid in the attic while her father tried to bribe them with anything they had—a few vegetables or small trinkets—so the family would be left alone. Sometimes at night they were disturbed by loud voices and knocking on the door. They wouldn't answer, hoping whoever it was would leave, rather than break in or set the house on fire.

If it was dangerous outside, it could often be just as desperate inside. Berlin's electricity and water systems were in shambles. In her diary, Ursula wrote that on April 21, 1945, "from about noon on there was no water anymore, for the past day and a half, no power." That meant no cooking, washing, listening to the radio, or reading after dark. Ursula wrote about not having oil for cooking or heating for two weeks and no meat for more than a month. When they finally got some, it was partly spoiled. Her family survived on the few vegetables and potatoes they could grow in their garden. Once, her family was so hungry they even ate squirrels her father had trapped. Meat was so scarce that by the end of the war, soldiers were eating the remaining animals from the Berlin Zoo—less than one hundred animals had survived the bombings and battles around them. The zoo, like the city itself, had gone from a place of international renown to one of ruin and tragic starvation.

On May 8, 1945, Germany surrendered to the Allied forces. The War was over. But that didn't mean that things would go back to normal for Ursula and her family, or for any other family. After all of the death and destruction caused by extreme antisemitic beliefs (hatred against Jews), things would never be "normal" again. Berlin was on edge. The Allied forces did not leave Germany. Instead, in an effort to stop any single country or leader from taking over the country, the Allies divided Germany into four zones. Each was controlled by one of the Allied powers: England, France, the United States, or the Soviet Union. Since Berlin was the capital of Germany, the city was divided into four zones too. If people wanted to go from one part of Berlin to another, they had to pass through military checkpoints guarded by armed soldiers.

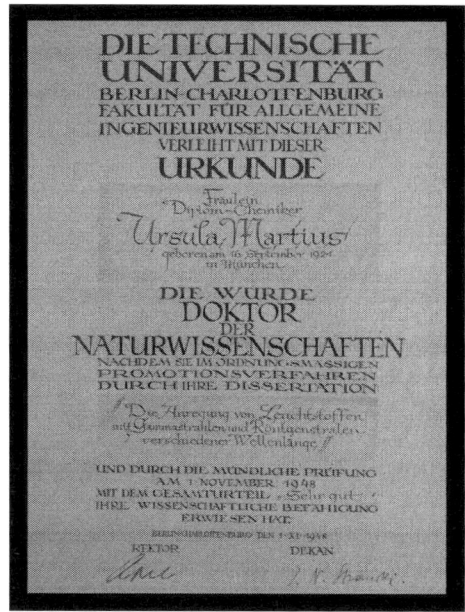

Ursula's diploma from the Technical University of Berlin, 1948.

The war may have destroyed a lot of things, but it didn't destroy Ursula's desire to learn. She was determined to continue her education. Under the terms of Germany's surrender, students who had been denied education by the Nazis could return to school with credit for the work they had completed before being forced to leave. This meant that Ursula could pick up where she had left off, but she decided not to return to the University of Berlin. It had too many bad memories for her.

Instead, she enrolled in the Technical University of Berlin. She had to get a special identification card so that she could cross from the French zone (where her house was), to the British zone (where the university was).

Just as she had done before the war, she studied physics. Even though she was already busy with her own schoolwork, Ursula readily agreed to supervise junior students and work as a research assistant for one of her professors. She saw both extra tasks as opportunities. Her special interest was how natural objects, such as crystals and rocks, form and behave over time. She was interested in how the smallest parts of these objects—molecules and atoms—worked together to create a whole object. It was very much the way, as a little girl, she learned how small shapes fit together to create bigger shapes. Ursula began to think about this as a way of looking at the world: like atoms or molecules that make up an object, humans have to work together to make a strong, healthy society.

While Ursula was finishing her studies, conditions grew worse in Berlin. People were starving: all food and supplies were stopped from entering the city because the four occupying countries were competing for control. The "Berlin Blockade" started in March 1948 and lasted almost a year. It caused great hardship to the citizens who were already struggling to pick up the pieces of their lives.

Having endured so much discrimination and terror for so long, Ursula was absolutely determined to finish her education. As long as she was allowed to walk into the school building and do her work, there was nothing that could scare her off. She passed her exams and graduated with a PhD in November of 1948. I keep her diploma on the wall of my home office in Toronto. It says that her overall standing was "*sehr gut*" (very good), but to me, it says far more about the young woman my mother was.

Ursula wanted to stay in Germany after graduation. With so many bad memories and broken relationships, I thought starting over somewhere new might have been an enticing relief. But Ursula saw another possibility. She wanted to help rebuild. As things improved, people dared to imagine what the country could be now that they were free of the Nazis. Germany began to open up again. Visiting professors and lecturers came from Europe and North America, bringing talk of innovation. People felt more optimistic and believed that great things could rise from the ashes.

It took Ursula a while to come to a sad realization. Universities could not lead the efforts to rebuild. Their directors and staff weren't open to new ways of thinking because they had been educated under the Nazi regime. All they could imagine for the future was what they were familiar with. Ursula wrote a short article saying just that, and it was published in a Berlin newspaper. Even though speaking up could put her in danger or damage her chances of work, Ursula had strong views. Fear was not about to hold her back from expressing them.

Just as they had done before the war, her thoughts turned to leaving the country. Ursula wrote to a friend of her mother who worked at Oxford University in England. That friend passed her name to others until finally, it caught some attention. The head of the Department of Physics at the University of Toronto (U of T) in Canada was looking for someone in her area of study: applied physics. Mom was offered the job.

However, having a job waiting for her was not enough. Many countries at the time, including Canada, had strict laws around immigration. They would only allow certain people from certain countries in. After the war, it was difficult for Germans to immigrate because they were still seen as the enemy. German Jews and "half-Jews," like Ursula, had to prove to the Canadian government that they had jobs and would be able to support themselves financially. Luckily, the University of Toronto connected Ursula to a financial program that would help her. The Canadian program specifically helped outstanding European scientists and scholars to come, settle, and work. Out of thirty-two refugees who received the Lady Davis Fellowship that year, my mother was the only woman.

The Lady Davis Foundation Report, 1949.

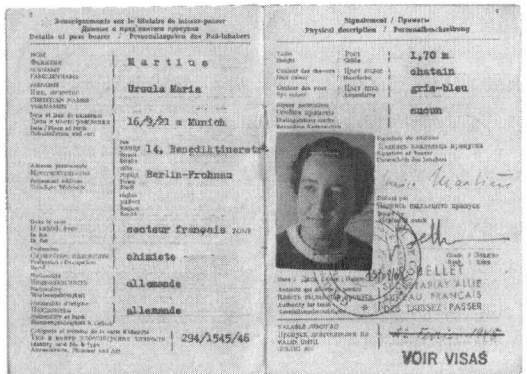

Ursula's Zonal Travel Permit for occupied Germany that she used to travel between the French and British zones of Berlin in post-war Germany.

Mom left Germany in 1949. She would return only once, for a short visit as part of a peace delegation in 1969. I was ten or eleven years old at the time. She had told me she was nervous about going back to Germany after so many years and was having nightmares. But after the trip, she said she should not have worried. Berlin felt like a completely different city by then. It had been entirely rebuilt after the war, and there was little that looked familiar to her. Mom said she found it almost reassuring that Berlin felt like any other European city. It must have been strange though, to go back to a city that held so much personal history and heartbreak and not find any familiar signs of them. Places where she'd gone to school, played in the park, and enjoyed outings with her parents just didn't exist anymore.

Ursula arrived in Canada on February 6, 1949. She was twenty-seven years old and completely alone in a foreign country. Her parents had remained in Berlin with the promise that Ursula would bring them to live with her in Toronto as soon as she could, but that wouldn't happen for several years. This was the beginning of a whole new chapter in Ursula's life.

# Part II

Early Years in Canada

# Chapter 4

# Ursula the Newcomer

Ursula browses the baked goods at a store near her rooming house. She has an empty basket on one arm. Nothing looks familiar. Nothing tastes familiar, either. All the bread here is white: white bread to slice and put in the toaster. Frowning, Ursula squints at the loaves on display. The storekeeper behind the counter says something to her, but he speaks so fast, she can't understand him. She shakes her head and sighs, leaving the shop empty-handed. She should have known better than to go to a regular store. Determined, she walks down to Harbord Bakery, a well-known Jewish shop. There she'll find rye bread with caraway seeds—a welcome taste of home.

In February 1949, my mother arrived in a city completely unlike the one she had just left. Although Berlin had been all but destroyed during the war, Ursula held on to her childhood memories of it as a thrilling urban metropolis filled with museums and galleries, artists and intellectuals. It had been everything you could dream a city could be. Toronto at the time was very different—it almost didn't feel like a city at all. For starters, it was small—the population of Toronto was about one third of Berlin's.

Queen Street, Toronto, 1950, during the construction of Toronto's first subway.

Most of the buildings were quite small too. Many of them were recently built, not at all like the historical streetscapes of Berlin. Toronto didn't even have subways or a good bus system. There weren't a lot of concerts or theaters to go to. It seemed to her that the only thing anyone could do was go to church. In some parts of the city, there was one on every corner! The strangest thing of all was how daily life seemed to stop on Sundays: by law, all the stores, businesses, and banks had to close so that Christians could attend church. Outside the main downtown area, Toronto was still quite rural, and some parts only had dirt roads. Ursula must have felt like a visitor on a strange, new planet. And in some ways, she was.

At home after the fighting, devastation was everywhere. But Canadians had experienced the war differently. The conflict took place overseas, not on Canadian soil. And although almost 45,400 Canadian soldiers died in the fighting, civilians here hadn't lived in cities that had been repeatedly bombed. Nor had they nearly starved to death or been surrounded by soldiers and countrymen who wanted to kill them. Very few Torontonians understood the kind of terror Ursula had known. It had left its mark deep within her.

In her early years in Toronto, Ursula lived as cheaply as she could, saving her money to bring her parents to Canada. She rented a small room on the third floor of a house on Walmer Road, near the University of Toronto. Ursula shared a kitchen and bathroom with the other renters—probably women who studied and worked at the university too. Being surrounded by students and staff might have made it easy

Queen Street West, 1953.

to make friends. But like a lot of newcomers to Canada, Ursula still had to learn a new language. She did have some English and could talk about science and physics, but she quickly found she needed to know everyday English. People spoke so fast that she couldn't understand them. She longed to have the right words to tell a storekeeper exactly what she wanted, to chat with a neighbor, or simply to find out where to put her trash on garbage days. Being a determined person, Ursula learned English quickly, so she could fit in as much possible.

Yet, it was a very lonely time for her with no family or friends to turn to. It was unusual for a single woman to come to Canada by herself. Most women who immigrated came to join husbands, fiancés, or family members. And while Canada is now a very multicultural country, when Ursula arrived there weren't many people like her. The population was quite small in 1950, just 13.7 million. Government officials understood the important role immigrants could play in building up the country, but they mostly wanted people from Western Europe, like Italians and Portuguese. Very few Jewish immigrants were allowed in after the Second World

War. Even though the Nazis had done horrific things to Jews, the rest of the world didn't view them as people in need of help and support. Instead, they continued to discriminate against them. The Canadian government, like many others in Europe as well as the United States, refused to allow entry to displaced Jews. If Ursula hadn't come to Canada with a job at the university and the Lady Davis Fellowship, her application almost certainly would have been refused.

It might be surprising that my mother didn't feel much of a connection to the Jewish population in Toronto, even though she had been labeled "half Jewish" and been punished for it. Since her family had not been part of the Jewish community in Germany, Ursula didn't have much interest in exploring her Jewish roots. In fact, her experiences during the war led her to be distrustful of *all* organized religions. She had seen enough of how religion can divide people into different factions; the "in" group that gets rewarded and the "out" group that gets punished. When divisions like this are created, they can quickly lead to one group being harmed or mistreated by the other. Ursula wanted something different. Something where everyone was respected, regardless of their beliefs. Something that united everyone in the common goal of making the world a better place. I don't know if she realized it, or had the English word for it, but what Ursula wanted was *activism*.

# Chapter 5

# Ursula the Scientist

Ursula is about to begin her day's work in the lab. On a table, a stack of rock samples awaits, each one carefully labeled with the location where it was collected. She puts one on a slide under the microscope. The sample is from deep within the Canadian Shield, the ancient rock formation that covers roughly half of the country. Ursula is trying to figure out just how old it really is. Peering into the eyepiece, she zooms in on the tiny, microscopic particles—the crystals and individual grains that are the building blocks of all rock life. She is looking for chemicals, the naturally occurring radioactive elements within the rocks: tritium, carbon 14, strontium 90. In a spiral notebook, she records the data.

Once settled into her new city, Ursula was ready to hunker down and focus on her work in the Department of Physics. Nothing would get in the way of her determination to learn as much as she could and find a way to benefit the world. It probably helped that there were few distractions: she was a young single woman, new to the country, without friends or family.

In the 1950s, not many women were involved in science, engineering, medicine, law, or architecture. When they were allowed to go to university, they tended to study languages and the humanities (such as history or philosophy), or household sciences (such as nutrition and cooking). Ursula was often the only woman in the lab, but that didn't bother her. In fact, she was used to being one of the few women in her entire field of research. Whenever her male peers resented her, Ursula ignored them. She was there to do her research. If she had to be the first woman to do it, then she would pave the way for others to come after her.

Most of the male students studied math and science, and particularly engineering. When Ursula first started work at U of T, many of the professors and students in engineering were, or had been, soldiers. The government paid for returning soldiers to go to university. They also gave money to universities for each soldier enrolled in their institutions. Female students who had started university during the war were often forced to leave to make room for the returning soldiers. The government and mainstream society at the time believed that women didn't need higher education because their so-called duty in life was to become wives and mothers. My mother's place was secure because her formal studies were over, and she was now doing research with her peers and the professors at the university. Still, I can't help but think my mother saw how unfair it was that more women weren't given opportunities to receive an education.

In universities, engineering departments often have strong ties to the military. In the past, this was partly because there were so many returning soldiers. It was also because the military viewed university

The Wallberg Building on the U of T campus opened in 1949. It was where Ursula began her work at the university and where she would spend a major part of her career.

engineering departments as part of the military, where new weapons and military techniques could be created and tested. The universities strongly supported the military. In the post-war years, it was considered a mark of national loyalty. The government and many private donors often gave funding to help military research.

Ursula did not support this. She had experienced how war destroyed her city and her country, and she wasn't going to be part of something that caused more destruction. Instead, she worked in experimental physics,

The Canadian Shield covers roughly half of Canada and is rich in natural resources. Minerals such as copper, gold, iron, silver, lead, uranium, zinc, as well as diamonds can be found in its different regions. Its numerous ecosystems are homes to boreal forests, the Arctic tundra, thousands of lakes and rivers and a rich diversity of wildlife. Rocks taken from the northern shore of Hudson's Bay are estimated to be 4.28 billion years old!

testing theories about matter and energy. This reminded Ursula of the puzzles she'd enjoyed as a child, figuring out how the pieces all fit together. Each experiment revealed something new and helped researchers understand more about the objects they were studying. For my mother, this kind of work was creative rather than destructive.

Ursula's specialty was the study of crystals. This field is helpful to many of the sciences. For example, it can be used in geology, the study of rocks. At U of T, Ursula worked closely with Dr. Edward Bullard, the head of the Physics Department. He was researching the Canadian Shield, a large rock formation that stretches across much of Canada. Dr. Bullard's team wanted to know how old it was. Ursula's role was to examine the minerals and chemicals in rocks that had been collected from different parts of the Shield. Using a microscope and X-rays, she could examine the patterns or molecules that made up each of the samples. Then she compared one sample to another. For example, a rock from the surface of the Shield would be different from a rock found deeper within it. Ursula studied the radioactive elements in the rocks. She knew how fast radiation breaks down over time. This was an important clue in determining how old the rocks were.

Ursula's knowledge of crystals could also be used in chemistry, medicine, or pharmacy. She was particularly interested in studying materials such as metals, ceramics, bones, or cloth to see how their properties changed with time and use. Ursula and the other researchers had to figure out the best methods and tools for gathering information. Mom told me she really enjoyed doing the lab work and then seeing how it was used to look at bigger questions about the world. It was ground-breaking, and Mother was showing everyone that women could be part of it.

After Ursula's fellowship at the University of Toronto ended in 1952, she took a full-time job at the Ontario Research Foundation (ORF), now called Ortech Industries. Companies and people who used a lot of machinery could seek help if they were having problems with their machines or products. Ursula was in charge of the X-ray lab and testing facilities. It was another opportunity for her to show how looking at something under a microscope could be applied

Ursula at her microscope while working for the Ontario Research Foundation.

to something bigger: solving a real-life workplace problem by analyzing the tiniest pieces.

Our mother used to tell Martin and me about some of the interesting cases from her ORF days. One time she examined equipment used in Arctic exploration to see how it was affected by the cold, harsh environment. The lab also examined the ropes and cables used in metal cages that lower miners underground. They wanted to understand how the ropes were affected by the conditions there. In these two cases alone, Ursula was helping to create more reliable equipment and machinery, which meant that people would be safer while they did their jobs.

Because she had become a specialist in her field, Ursula was invited to partner with the Royal Ontario Museum (ROM), one of the largest museums in Canada. The ROM asked Ursula whether she could use X-rays to determine the age of some of their oldest objects. Because many of the museum's objects were extremely precious, they couldn't allow tests that might destroy or damage them. Ursula agreed to try, and thus began a partnership with the ROM that would continue for many years. She would go on to use X-ray techniques and nondestructive testing not only to date ancient objects, but also to learn how and where they were made, and by whom.

Ursula's childhood fascination with ancient objects and cultures continued in Canada! Over time, she would develop new ways to learn even more about them.

# Chapter 6

# Ursula the Mother

The sun shines bright in their backyard. Ursula lays out plates while Monica plays in the small sandbox and Martin climbs the apple tree with his father's help. A loud noise splits the air, and two fighter jets zoom over their heads. The air show marks the end of the Canadian National Exhibition every year. The sound is so loud you can feel it in your stomach. Ursula and her husband both startle and duck. Ursula's heart races just as fast as the planes in the sky. She remembers all too vividly the planes that flew over Berlin, dropping bomb after bomb upon the city until it lay in ruins.

Mom met my father, Fred Franklin, at a small musical get-together held by some fellow German music lovers. Fred had been born and raised in Germany too, and his mother, like Ursula's, was of Jewish ancestry. Unlike Ursula, Fred had been able to get out of Germany about two years before the Second World War began. At the age of fifteen, he was sent to a boarding school in Sussex, England. It was not an easy time for him. He missed his family terribly, and he told us that his teachers would strike him with a leather strap for speaking German. Fred spent the war years in England and was able to come to Canada in 1948 by working in the engine room of the *Queen Mary*, a large British ocean liner.

Fred was quite an adventurer! After arriving in Canada, he hitchhiked across the country from the East to the West Coast. There, he worked on boats that delivered food and supplies to the Gulf Islands. Later, he worked in a sawmill. Finally, he came to Toronto to take a job at an engineering company. Fred was very musical: he played recorder and cello. He and Ursula bonded over their love of music.

After meeting at the musical event, my mom and dad gradually got to know each other. Like Ursula, Fred was close to his parents and was saving his money to bring them to Canada. They also shared many of the same beliefs: they were against war and knew the importance of actively making the world a better place. Most importantly, Fred supported Ursula's ambitions.

Ursula and Fred, circa 1952, shortly after they were married.

Mom and Dad married on May 2, 1952. It was a small wedding, with just a few friends. The couple moved into a little apartment in the Forest Hill area of Toronto and eventually were able to send for their parents in Germany. Then they bought a house in downtown Toronto, where my brother and I grew up.

Ursula's colleagues at the Ontario Research Foundation were shocked when she told them she was pregnant. The ORF had never had a woman scientist before, so they'd never had to deal with a pregnant employee!

In Ontario at this time, there were no laws around maternity leave. As far as the government and much of society were concerned, most women didn't work anyway, and if they did, they would quit their jobs when they started a family. The culture of the 1950s made it seem like men were always the "breadwinners" or money-earners in their households. In reality, many women worked all kinds of jobs, whether they were single or married, had children or not. This was especially true for women from working-class backgrounds who didn't have wealthy families or highly paid husbands to support them. Not only that, during the war, women had taken many jobs that needed to be filled when the men went off to fight. It was considered patriotic. But when the war ended, those same women were expected leave their jobs and return home. They were supposed to be doting wives and mothers—not employees!

The government didn't create laws around maternity leave until the 1970s, after many years of feminist activism. So, women had to figure things out for themselves in a system that wasn't designed to support them. Ursula told her colleagues at the ORF that she wanted to continue working after her child was born. She skipped her summer holidays while she was pregnant so that she could take three weeks off when Martin was born in 1955. After those three weeks, she returned to work part-time. Ursula did the same when I came along in 1958.

My brother and I were born at Women's College Hospital in Toronto. I was thrilled when I found out! Before it was founded, becoming a doctor in Canada was almost impossible for women, because universities refused to accept them as students. In the 1880s, a group of suffragettes, women demanding equal rights, petitioned the mayor of Toronto to open a school where women could study medicine. Women's College Hospital became a place for female doctors and students to train and do research, and where female patients could get medical care from women doctors.

For me, being born there proved that my mother knew how important it was to support other women, especially those who worked in male-dominated fields, like she did. Her support was not just talk; it was action. While many people believed that women doctors were not as capable as their male counterparts, Ursula trusted them. She placed her own health care, and her children's, in their hands.

Mom was able to go back to work after we were born because our grandmother was there to help take care of us. Ilse had come to Canada from Germany in 1950, but our grandfather did not come at the same time. It would take two more years before Albrecht was allowed to join us. Both my parents had to work to support themselves, my brother and me, as well as all four of our grandparents. Like many

Holocaust survivors, Ursula's parents were in poor health, with both mental and physical ailments. Fred's parents had been in an internment camp. Even though they had managed to get to England and lived there before the war, in the mid-1940s they were put in an internment camp on the Isle of Wight.

Ursula, Martin, and Monica, Dec. 1959.

An internment camp is similar to a prison, except the people there haven't broken any rules. The government considers them to be political enemies and locks them up. Fred's parents were considered "enemy aliens." They had been born in Germany, and since England was at war with Germany, Germans were seen as enemies. My father, in contrast, was a "friendly alien" because he had gone to school in England. He was allowed to work and was even a block captain during the bombings in Birmingham. He guided people into shelters at the sound of the warning sirens. He told us that one day he went to work and saw the streetcar rails standing straight up in a crater that a bomb had created the night before!

Even though Mom did her best to leave the past behind her, Martin and I caught glimpses of how the war had impacted her. We found out things by "reading between the lines," picking up on things our mother said or did. She always startled easily and hated loud, sudden noises, like a car backfiring or fireworks. Both Mom and Dad hated the annual air show at the Canadian National Exhibition, with its patriotic flag-waving and loud fighter jets overhead. It brought back memories of living in cities that had been bombed during the war—Ursula in Berlin and my father in Birmingham, England. Mother disliked all efforts to "normalize" war, or make it seem heroic or glamorous. Her thoughts were always with the civilians. They are the ones who truly have to deal with the worst impacts of military conflicts.

Because my father was so supportive of Mom's career, he helped at home when she returned to full-time work. When Martin and I were still young, it was our dad who was there when we came home from school. He'd left his job and started his own business making musical instruments in his garage workshop.

We all lived very simply and frugally. Mom and Dad never wasted food. They bought day-old bread and meat-ends that nobody else wanted, and they shopped from bargain bins. My parents rarely bought new things, and they would wear clothes and shoes until they fell apart. We went on very few family vacations, and when we did, we camped. We didn't have a television set until I was a teenager, but I don't recall missing anything. We read a lot, and the house was always full of activity, books, newspapers, ideas, and talk, especially about making the world a better place.

# Part III

Forging Her Own Path

# Chapter 7

# Ursula the Feminist

Ursula finds herself at the Canadian National Exhibition. It's not a place she really wants to be. The noises of the midway games and rides, shouts of thrill-seekers, cries of tired children, and the movement of the crowd are almost overwhelming. But Ursula is on a mission. She and a group of women have rented a booth here. A banner with the group's name Voice of Women waves in the breeze. As people pass by, Ursula hands out pamphlets: THE DANGERS OF NUCLEAR WEAPONS is in bold letters at the top.

Next to the booth is a barrel filled with small teeth—children's teeth. Ursula knows this will catch attention—it is a barrel full of teeth, after all—but she's happy to explain it. Throughout the day, many children visit the booth to drop off their baby teeth, saved for weeks, or even months. Ursula thanks them and hands each child a sticker that reads, "I gave my tooth to science!"

Now that Ursula had been living in Canada for over ten years, she felt less like a newcomer and more like part of a growing network of family, friends, and colleagues.

Between work and home, life was busy. It would have been easy to quietly follow a daily routine and let life fly by. But Mom could never ignore things happening around her, whether they were in her own backyard or in the world at large.

Around this time, the US and the Soviet Union were locked in the Cold War. Almost every time Ursula opened a newspaper, she was greeted with gloomy images of human suffering and unsettling articles about the threat of war. With a pit in the bottom of her stomach, Ursula read how the two opposing sides (and their allies) were gathering more and more weapons to threaten each other with. By the 1960s, both governments had become so focused on proving how powerful they were that they had gathered enough nuclear weapons to destroy the whole planet. Both the United States and the Soviet Union had been creating and testing nuclear weapons since the Second World War. And both sides absolutely knew that nations using nuclear weapons against each other would cause unimaginable damage. Yet, neither side seemed willing to back down. It made Ursula sad and angry too. Why couldn't people learn from all the pain and destruction caused by the Second World War? Why would anyone want to go through that again?

> A *cold war* happens when countries threaten to fight each other but never actually do. The US and the Soviet Union were almost equal in strength, and each wanted to prevent the other from gaining too much power. Both countries had allies—it was like the world was divided in two. Each side had gathered a large number of weapons to frighten the other, although neither really wanted to use them. They knew that if one side used the weapons, the other would too, and the result would be terrible.

The catastrophic possibilities of the Cold War had already been demonstrated in 1941. After Japan attacked the American Navy stationed at Pearl Harbor (off the Hawaiian Island of Oahu), the US retaliated by dropping an atomic bomb on Hiroshima and another on Nagasaki. Most of the people in both large cities were killed or horribly wounded. The chemical radiation left behind by these bombs would impact the health of survivors for generations to come.

Because Canada was an ally of the US, Canadians were afraid they could be pulled into a conflict between the two superpowers. There were US weapons and military bases in Canada that might make Canada a target. The world was becoming aware that health was being affected by nuclear weapon testing over North America and the Pacific. Newspapers reported that when nuclear weapons exploded in the air, they released radioactive materials and gases into the atmosphere. How much of this fell down to the earth, and how did the fallout affect people and nature? Nobody knew.

Ursula had already lived through the horrors of bombs and mass murders during the war, and it was unacceptable—impossible—for her to do nothing. She was a pacificist and believed that conflicts between people and countries could be solved without violence. She also knew that the leaders in charge of making decisions about wars are rarely the ones who are most affected by them. During a war, it's always the ordinary people who suffer the most. Ursula felt that she needed to be a voice for people who could not speak for themselves. The question for her was: where could she go to share and spread her ideas?

In 1960, Lotta Dempsey, one of the few women journalists of the time, wrote a newspaper article in the *Toronto Star*, stating that if men could not figure out how to stop the Cold War, perhaps women could! The response from women was overwhelming. A huge public meeting took place, which led to the formation of Voice of Women (VOW). VOW was a feminist organization for Canadian women who wanted to stand up against violence, war, and nuclear weapons. When Ursula heard about the group, she joined to provide herself with a platform from which she could make change.

All VOW members were volunteers who were willing to take a stand for their beliefs. Ursula was right there with them and one of the few who had a scientific background. She would help by applying her scientific knowledge and expertise to solve real-life, practical problems, just as she was doing in her job at the ORF. The problem to solve? How to prevent nuclear war!

Ursula became VOW's director of research; she was in charge of educating the public about radiation. She knew that when people understand the causes of

> In the 1960s more and more people across North America and the world were beginning to insist on their rights and the rights of the planet. The issues were plentiful: Feminism, African American and Black Canadian civil rights, LGBTQ+ rights, Indigenous rights, rights for the disabled, water pollution, and a warming planet were among them. People wanted to live safe, fulfilling lives, to practice and celebrate their cultures, to openly love and/or marry whomever they wished, to go where they wished, and to work where they wished. People were working to create the greater freedoms they dreamed of. Sometimes their demonstrations were frowned upon or ignored, but little by little, voices began to be heard and issues started to be addressed.

The Voice of Women protest against the war in Vietnam.

problems they face in life, they are more able to find solutions to them. And when more people see others working to come up with solutions, they realize they can contribute too. In other words, activism makes knowledge more accessible to people from all walks of life.

Ursula already knew a lot about radiation from the work she did at U of T. She had looked at the radiation that formed and decayed naturally in rocks from the Canadian Shield. Now she started to investigate the radiation that fell to earth as a result of nuclear testing.

Scientists were aware that when someone is exposed to radiation, it builds up in their body and can lead to cancer. What they didn't know very much about was the radiation that resulted from testing nuclear weapons. They generally believed that it probably stayed in the upper atmosphere and did not fall down to earth. But Ursula and the VOW wanted to test this theory. If the radiation *did* fall down to earth, it would stay in the soil and contaminate plants that grew there. It was possible that people and animals would end up with radiation in their bodies when they ate these plants. This was a big worry.

VOW decided to do a detailed study. Under Ursula's guidance, it would focus on strontium 90, a radioactive element that could be found and measured not only in rocks, but in bones and teeth. Ursula led a study that would look at children's teeth. Measuring the amount of strontium 90 in a child's tooth would show how much radiation had built up in the body from the time the child's tooth first started to grow until it fell out, approximately six years later. Since so little radiation is found naturally in the human body, this would be a scientific way to see if children were being infected by the fallout from nuclear testing.

To carry out their study, VOW members from across Canada had to collect baby teeth. They started with their own children's, but soon women from all across the country were mailing teeth to Toronto. Schools, libraries, churches, and dentists got involved too. From 1962 to 1964, VOW collected about six thousand teeth! Martin still remembers his teeth being "donated" to the campaign. Whenever he lost a tooth, he would leave it under the pillow for the tooth fairy, but somehow the tooth ended up in the VOW study!

Mother decided it was best to send all the teeth to a government lab for analysis. She thought the results would be seen as more objective or scientific if she and the lab at U of T weren't involved. The analysis was done in an official government lab where testing was carried out for all the doctors in Ontario.

"VOW Puts Teeth Into Plans," a newspaper article from *The Telegram* on March 15, 1963, about the collection of baby teeth used to measure radioactive material.

What happened next? No one seems to know. Maybe the tests never took place. If they did, the results were kept secret. Ursula was convinced the teeth *were* analyzed and the results showed that Canadian children had high levels of radiation in their bodies. She was also convinced that government officials didn't want this made public because they were afraid more people would protest nuclear testing. She may have been right. But even without the test results, there was more and more public protest against nuclear testing. VOW believed that their work contributed to Canada signing a temporary nuclear test ban in 1963.

Ursula's involvement in VOW and the baby teeth campaign shaped her life and work. She found a community in the feminist movement, and she often spoke about the atmosphere of cooperation and collaboration she found there: everyone had a part to play. It was important to her that their activism was based on regular women working together on a task. As with the baby teeth study, they were early "citizen scientists": people whose observations of things in their daily life contributed important information to trained scientists. Ursula believed that everyone should play a part in identifying problems and solving them because they are the ones who have the most to gain or lose. Such important decisions should not be left to the so-called experts. This was an important concept for Ursula, one that she would keep coming back to throughout her life.

> **Our Milk Reported Worst Hit By Fallout**
>
> By LEONARD BERTIN
> Star Science Editor
>
> Radioactive contamination of Canadian milk last year hit levels three times higher than in any of eight other major countries that carried out regular tests, according to a report compiled and released by Voice of Women.
>
> Further "major fall-out effects" can be expected this summer as a result of tests carried out by the U.S. and Russia in 1961-62, the report says. These equalled in amount all previous nuclear tests.
>
> The fall-out figures are from published reports and have been declared by authorities in Canada, the U.S. and Britain to be far below danger level.
>
> The report, submitted to Judy LaMarsh, federal health minister, says Canada does less about radioactive fall-out than other leading countries like Britain, the United States and Western Germany. But dangers are often much greater, because of our geographic position, it says.
>
> The report was compiled by VOW's research committee, headed by Dr. Ursula Franklin, a University of Toronto lecturer who is in charge of the x-ray department of the Ontario Research Foundation.

"Our Milk Reported Worst Hit by Fallout," newspaper article from the *Toronto Star*.

# Chapter 8

# Ursula the Quaker

Ursula, her husband, and their children hold hands as they wind through the crowd. They don't want to get separated on the International Peace Bridge, which crosses the border between Canada and the US. Ursula nods and smiles at familiar faces, people she knows from the Quaker meetings back in Toronto. She smiles at all the new, friendly faces too. Some kids carry balloons, and adults hold signs in the air. It feels like a party, but it isn't. It's a protest.

Quakers are members of a Christian religion that, among other things, believe strongly in nonviolence. Today, they've come together to protest the Vietnam War. With a jolt, Ursula notices the hundreds of police officers and military forces standing on the sidelines of the Peace Bridge. Ursula shakes her head at the irony. They are all standing on a bridge named for peace. The Quakers are here promoting peace and carry no weapons. The police and military are here to keep the peace and they are armed with guns. *What's wrong with this picture?* Ursula wonders.

Some of the children are afraid. Despite her own nervousness in front of uniformed soldiers and police, Ursula kneels down to comfort

George Fox, a founder of the Quakers, a Christian religious community that was originally founded in England some four hundred years ago. They are sometimes called The Religious Society of Friends, or just Friends for short. Over time, Quakers became known for their anti-war and anti-slavery efforts. In more recent years, they have participated in activism around prison reform, social justice, and international peace movements. While it may seem strange for a religious community to be so involved in activism, it really isn't. For instance, many leaders of the African American Civil Rights Movement drew inspiration and strength from their religious beliefs. Quakers believe that faith is not only about going to church on Sundays: it is also about what you do in your day-to-day life. This is why they are committed to taking action on social justice. Social justice is the belief that everyone is equal and deserving of the same rights, freedoms, and opportunities.

a young girl, reminding her that standing up for your beliefs can be scary, but you can't let that stop you.

In our family, Mom wasn't the only activist. My father, Fred, was an activist too. In fact, you could say that the whole family got involved in supporting our community. For Martin and me, donating our teeth to science was just one little part of what it would mean to grow up in a household that was strongly against war and violence. Because they had experienced the horrors of war firsthand, both of our parents knew that violent battles had terrible, long-term effects on everyone. They felt strongly that violence was not a good way to solve problems. It only created more problems. My parents wanted to surround our family with people who were interested in finding peaceful solutions to these problems. So, they sought out a religious, Christian environment in which to raise Martin and me, where we and our values could be supported. They found it in the Quakers.

My father had first learned about Quakers when he lived in England during the War. In the early 1960s, my parents attended their first Quaker meeting in Toronto. There, they found people whose beliefs matched their own. Quakerism was particularly appealing to Ursula because there were no leaders, ministers, priests, or rabbis. There is no one "in charge" because Quakers believe there is a part of

God in everyone. Each person is respected regardless of who they are or what their background is. And very importantly, Quakers are opposed to war and violence, just like Ursula and Fred were.

Mom and Dad quickly got involved in the Canadian Friends Service Committee, which is the "social and political action" part of the Quakers. A major activity at that time was protesting the war in Vietnam. It had been raging on since 1955. What started as a civil war between North and South Vietnam took a deadlier turn when the US got involved to support South Vietnam. The Americans dropped bomb after bomb on the country and spread highly poisonous chemicals into the forests and farmlands. Many civilians died, as did many soldiers on both sides of the fighting.

A huge difference between the Vietnam War and previous conflicts was that most families in North America now had televisions at home. Every night on the news, people watched as bombs dropped on Vietnam and as civilians were killed in the streets. With earlier wars, you would only hear about things weeks or even months after they had happened. The Vietnam War was playing out in real time in living rooms everywhere. It was impossible to ignore.

Like many Canadians, the Quakers were against the war and Canada's role in it. Canada did not send troops to fight, but it depended on American dollars to support its manufacturing, mining, and fossil fuel industries, so it sold "raw war materials" to the US. Quaker activism took many forms. They organized educational events and wrote to the government. They also took part in

The Peace Bridge, where Monica remembers protesting the Vietnam War as a child with her family.

big, international protests. Martin and I remember attending an event on the Peace Bridge between Canada and the United States. Peace activists from both countries came together on this symbolic monument to protest the war. For us as kids, it was exciting. We sang along with the music, grabbed cookies and cupcakes someone had brought, and played tag with our friends. But the adults, especially my parents, must have been very aware of the armed police and military officers everywhere.

The Quakers also acted in quieter ways; ways that had to be kept secret. For example, at that time young American men were forced by law to sign up for the military when they turned eighteen. In other words, they were drafted. Many of them came to Canada because they did not want to fight in the Vietnam War. The Quakers in Canada worked at finding "draft dodgers" places to live, work, and study.

I remember Mother speaking at the University of Toronto, supporting a student group that opposed the war. She wrote lots of letters to politicians and newspapers and attended protests and demonstrations. Mom was also active in the Quaker campaign to provide medical aid and supplies to civilians on *both* sides of the conflict.

Ursula's faith and her place in the Quaker community were fundamental to her. The Quakers gave her an outlet for living a life that reflected her values. She saw many similarities between Quakerism and the Voice of Women. The two most important to her were the spirit of cooperation and the focus on ordinary people. Mother even saw some familiar faces from VOW in the Quaker meetings! The people in the feminist community and the Quaker community became her friends and allies. They would support Mother in her various career struggles and challenges at the university, and in Canadian society. In return, she actively helped both communities to grow and succeed in their goals.

# Chapter 9

# Ursula the Professor

Ursula walks down the hall, trying to hide her jittery nerves. It's the first day of the school year, and professors have to be prepared for pranks from their students. Ursula's first-year engineering students will almost certainly try to surprise her. A snake in her desk drawer, maybe? A frog in the pocket of her lab coat? Perhaps a smoke bomb? One year, a bucket of water drenched her from above when she walked into the classroom! A woman professor is an oddity to a classroom full of men. They have a hard time believing she has the right—or the knowledge—to stand in front of them as their teacher. *One day*, she thinks, *I will not be the only one. There will be women teaching and studying in engineering departments everywhere.* But not today. She opens the classroom door, takes a deep breath, and steps in.

In 1967, Ursula became a full-time associate professor in U of T's Faculty of Engineering. She was the first woman professor in the Department of Metallurgical Engineering, which is all about understanding metals, how they work, and what we can do with them. Her appointment was a sign that the university's attitudes toward women in science were beginning to change…slowly.

When our mother returned to work full-time, I was nine years old and Martin was twelve. Even then, we knew our family was unusual. My brother and I tried to hide it. In the 1960s, most kids, especially those from immigrant families, wanted to fit in and be the same as everyone else. I may have been the only girl in my class whose mother worked outside the home. The kind of work she did was also unusual. I remember having a big argument about it with a teacher once. Somewhat as a joke, I had completed a form that asked for my parents' names and occupations. Beside Mother's name, I wrote "Prof. Eng." The teacher insisted that the abbreviation meant "Professor of English" rather than "Professional Engineer" (as I had intended), because only men could be engineers! My father was also considered unusual. Fathers of the kids in my class worked downtown, but mine worked from home. He was the "house parent" in our family.

By this time, we had moved to our home near Yonge and St. Clair. Some of my earliest memories are of hurried breakfasts on school days and Mother rushing out of our house to catch the bus to work. Sometimes she was so distracted that she left still wearing an apron! On those days, I ran after her to grab the apron before she got on the bus. Sometimes I managed to catch her, but not always. I think Maria, the department's secretary, also kept an eye out for the apron in case she needed to remove it before Ursula stood in front of the class.

Mother taught all levels of engineering students, from first-year students to PhD candidates. She liked teaching, but it was challenging because almost all of the students were men, many of whom didn't like being taught by a woman. Simply because they wore trousers, the men felt Ursula had nothing of value to teach them. It wasn't only her students who felt this way. The whole Engineering Department was often resentful. The Engineering Society had a so-called humorous newsletter where aggressive and violent comments about women appeared, and Ursula was often the target of their anger.

Sometimes when we talk about misguided attitudes in the past, we say "that's just how things were back then." But that's not really true. The students who disrespected Ursula made the choice to behave that way, just as she made the choice not to be intimidated by them. After everything she had lived through, she wasn't about to let a group of misguided students frighten her.

In fact, as time went on, Ursula played a role in changing the atmosphere of intimidation within the department. More young women were becoming interested in studying engineering, but as "girls" they felt a lot of pressure to fit in. They sometimes thought they had to act like "one of the boys" or accept any negative comments and abuse that came their way. As someone who had unintentionally been "the first girl" for much of her life, Ursula understood the challenges that these young women would face. She supported them and spoke out against the sexist atmosphere. She also let women students know that they could come to her office if they wanted to talk or needed advice. Still, it would be a long time before there were significant numbers of female students in engineering. Only then would the climate really change.

Ursula's challenges at work didn't only come from her students. Her colleagues weren't always happy about her presence, either. She objected to the way her co-workers spoke about women students. She raised the issue to many of them privately and also at staff meetings. This didn't earn her many friends. Even the architecture of the university seemed like it was against her. The Engineering Department's staff meetings often took place at Hart House, a male-only athletic center on campus. Ursula had to get special permission just to enter the building! It wasn't until 1972 that women were finally allowed to be members of Hart House.

For the longest time, there was only one women's washroom in the building where Ursula worked—one washroom for all the women who worked there: professors, office support staff, and students. It was still like that in the 1990s when I would visit my mother's office as an undergraduate student.

Being a woman wasn't the only thing that made Ursula stand out. Even when it came to ideas about the goal of engineering, she was an outsider. Just as she had when she first came to the university as a researcher, she still believed it was wrong for the Engineering Department to be so closely connected to the military. But much of the money spent on research came from government, businesses, and

A staff meeting in 1953. Only four of the professors photographed are women.

the armed forces. When these entities gave "gifts" of money, they wanted to know what it was being spent on. They might expect the research to go toward creating things like "better" weapons or oil drills to take fuel out of the earth faster, without considering the impact on the environment.

This was a major problem for Ursula. She took a stand against the use of military funding in the department and against research that could be used by the military in times of war. She spoke out in staff meetings, objecting to accepting contracts from the military for classified (or secret) research. On principle, she said she would not apply for funding from the Department of Defence. This made Mother quite unpopular. Her colleagues felt that she was not loyal to the university or the country. The head of her department warned that her career would suffer and that she was depriving students of equipment and money needed for relevant training.

Students were told that they wouldn't be able to get good jobs if they did advanced courses with Ursula.

But the excellent quality of Ursula's teaching and research could not be denied. People had started to consider her an important scientist. And students did seek her out for advanced courses, sometimes because of her beliefs, sometimes in spite of them, because she was an excellent and knowledgeable teacher. Ursula was asked to join various university groups, particularly those about women in engineering and women faculties. As well, she was invited to join national organizations such as the Natural Sciences and Engineering Research Council and the National Research Council. She was even asked to be on the Atomic Energy Control Board! That invitation was quickly withdrawn a day later when they realized Ursula was strongly *against* atomic energy because of its link to atomic weapons.

As time passed, some of Mother's colleagues came to agree with her stance against accepting military donations. They saw how such "gifts" took away the independence of the researchers. And by accepting big donations from large corporations, it looked like the university approved of what the corporations were doing, even if those things were harmful.

So, while she may have been unusual and unpopular at times, Ursula's knowledge, hard work, and commitment to her values were eventually recognized and shared by others. Over time, she found a community within the university just as she had with the Voice of Women and the Quakers. Now, she could join her voice with theirs. And she knew that when we join our voices together, we become even louder.

# Part IV

Making Connections

# Chapter 10

# Ursula the Activist

Ursula sits in a church basement looking around at all the women crowded together. A Vietnamese woman stands at the front of the room, and everyone is silent. The situation in Vietnam sounds so terrible and so desperate. What can Canadian women do to help? "What we really need," the woman explains, "are blankets and clothes for our babies. In dark colors only. Families are living underground in caves or in makeshift shelters. If their clothes are too bright, they might be seen by soldiers and jet bombers." The audience is horrified.

"I can help," someone says.

"I can ask my mother—she loves to knit," says another.

*I should learn to knit*, Ursula tells herself. *I'll find the time somehow. This is important. But surely we can do more! If everyone here writes letters to the government, talks to their neighbors, tells people what is happening in Vietnam, maybe things will change.*

For some years, the feminist and Quaker communities were like two separate threads of Mother's life. In different ways, they gave her a sense of strength and

Ursula Franklin, Muriel Duckworth (who was an active VOW member), and Monica Franklin, holding up a banner with a maple leaf and Japanese writing, showing their solidarity with the survivors of the 1945 atomic bomb attacks in Japan. There were two atomic bombs dropped at the end of the war: the first in Hiroshima and the second in Nagasaki. The nuclear fallout from these atomic bombs impacted people for decades after the bombs were dropped, causing many kinds of cancers and other health issues. (Photo circa 1975.)

a foundation to work from. When things happened around her that went against her beliefs, she spoke out more. One of Ursula's gifts was her ability to make connections between the communities, making them stronger. So, over time, Ursula began to weave these two threads together. She drew on the skills, knowledge, and values of each community to benefit everyone.

With the Voice of Women, Ursula raised public awareness around nuclear weapons and the dangers of radiation. The baby tooth study had been a good start, but the women of VOW couldn't stop there. Using her scientific knowledge, Ursula and other volunteers began to measure the amount of radiation in the foods people ate. Then they compared the results with the food from some other countries that were also doing nuclear testing. They discovered that Canadian milk had three times more radiation in it than any of the other countries' milk. That frightened people. Many VOW members switched their families from drinking fresh milk to powdered milk because they hoped it would be safer. I still remember how different it tasted and how much I disliked it! In 1969, my mother went to Ottawa with a VOW delegation to present the final brief to the Canadian government. To my knowledge, VOW never received a response.

VOW was also concerned about how war affected children. In the early 1960s, major department stores like Eaton's sold war toys: guns, tanks, and model soldiers. The stores created a lot of advertisements for these toys. The annual Eaton's

Christmas Catalogue had fourteen pages of them! VOW believed that these ads and toys made violence seem glamorous and exciting to kids. They also worried that such toys could encourage children to react to conflict with violence. My brother remembers how Mom forbade him from playing with toy tanks and guns and scolded him when he used a stick as a pretend gun. VOW led a protest against the toys and asked women to tear out the pages from the catalogues and mail them back to Eaton's. Thousands did.

VOW did their public protests and studies to get the government's attention. They wanted to put pressure on the Canadian government to make better decisions for its citizens. It turns out that the government was paying attention to VOW, but not always in a desirable way. In 2013, a researcher studying the history of VOW found that the Royal Canadian Mounted Police (RCMP) had files that listed details about the lives of many VOW members—including Ursula. The RCMP had watched and collected information about her from 1949 (when she came to Canada) until at least 1984. That's more than thirty years! Much of the file was related to her activism with VOW. The RCMP even had notes taken by spies who had attended VOW's regular monthly meetings and events! Later in life, Ursula would make sure that the RCMP's actions would not be forgotten. She insisted that her RCMP file be preserved forever in the collection of her papers at the University of Toronto Archives.

As a peace organization, VOW's biggest goal of all was to break down barriers between people and help them understand each other. They wanted to get rid of the "us versus them" attitude that is so common in conflicts and disagreements. To do this, VOW had to connect women from different walks of life and from differing sides of a conflict. They sent members to war-torn countries to talk to women about their experiences and hopes. In turn, VOW members welcomed international visitors to Canada. During the Cold War, they brought women from the United States and the Soviet Union together to discuss their struggles. Similarly, during the Vietnam War, they met with women from Vietnam, Laos, and the US to discuss how the war was impacting their lives. Later, they did the same with women

Ursula expressed her beliefs in the foreword to Maxine Kaufman-Lacusta's 2010 book, *Refusing to be Enemies: Palestinian and Israeli Nonviolent Resistance to the Israeli Occupation*. The book is made up of the changes that more than a hundred activists suggested were necessary for real peace in the region. The idea of "refusing to be enemies" appealed to Ursula. It says that people have choices. They can choose *not* to be enemies, *not* to allow themselves to be divided into groups pitted against one another. It says that people can be active rather than passive, working with others who may be different to build something better. Ursula supported the ideas and nonviolent strategies outlined in the book because they were creative and went beyond one side winning and the other losing. Finding ways that allowed everyone to gain, meant that there was less suffering and more justice for all.

from Israel and Palestine. They wanted those women to see that their "enemies" shared the same fears and concerns as they did. Meeting like this helped both sides of a conflict realize they had a common goal; to make the world a better place for their children and grandchildren. When differing sides of a disagreement can find common ground, they can often find a way to resolve the conflict. Also, working together with people makes it more difficult to see them as "the enemy."

This mission of breaking down barriers was something Ursula explored with the Quakers too. It's not easy to find nonviolent solutions to conflicts, so Ursula and the Quakers would have to develop techniques that could be used to decrease tension in violent situations. This is something they continue to explore in present-day conflicts such as the one in the Middle East.

Ursula read widely about Quakers and pacifism. She looked at how the roots of their beliefs determined the actions of early Quakers. Some had been imprisoned for their beliefs. Some joined the wartime Friends Ambulance Unit to provide medical treatment to civilians and soldiers on both sides of a conflict. Others refused to pay the portion of their taxes that went to the military, saying that the money should be used to promote peace. Using what she learned, Ursula gave speeches and wrote about nonviolence, peace, and social justice. Her audience wasn't just other Quakers or feminists—she wanted to reach people across the whole of Canada.

For Ursula, peace was not just the absence of war and fear—it was also the presence of justice. Peace was a commitment to the future. My mother used to say, "If you want peace, work for justice." She worked to spread this message as widely as she could.

Gathering with people to make positive change is exactly what Ursula had dreamed of when she was a young woman in Berlin. Then, she had hoped that she and other people from the universities could rebuild a better, more equal Germany. While she was never able to do that work in her home country, she certainly did in Canada.

In the 1960s, more young women were attending university and seeking jobs outside of the traditional female fields of teaching, nursing, and secretarial work. Ursula was especially passionate about supporting women who were working in male-dominated sectors like she did. But just as she had experienced herself, there were still many barriers for women. Everything from sexual harassment in the workplace to a lack of childcare support kept them away from certain jobs. Many felt like second-class citizens: they did the same work as men but didn't get the same pay or opportunities for advancement.

Feminists pushed the government to take action on this. In 1967, the Canadian government formed the Royal Commission on the Status of Women. The commission was made up of people who traveled across the country and met with women from factory workers to stay-at-home moms to women who worked in education, professions, and in business. Almost four years later, the commission's report was published. It revealed that discrimination against women was widespread, especially in law, medicine, and business.

The Royal Commission showed what Ursula had always known: she and other women who worked at the university were paid less than men. The fact that there were very few women in the higher ranks of the faculty meant that females were viewed as less capable and less deserving than their male coworkers. It proved that very few women were making decisions that affected all females at the university, and it gave Ursula the evidence she needed to one day take a stand on this.

By recording evidence, the commission had revealed a pattern of discrimination against women from the government and society in general. Besides providing evidence, the commission helped unite women across the country. It told them that their problems were real, and they were not alone with their difficulties. They were still struggling for respect. When they saw this, more women wanted to participate in taking action for themselves. They weren't going to wait for the men in government to do it for them.

It was just as Ursula had said all along—the power to change things was in the hands of common people who could work together toward a single goal.

# Chapter 11

# Ursula the Environmentalist

The sun sparkles off the lake as the children finish their swim races in the annual regatta. They make their way to the dock in front of the old cottage up high on the rocks. Ursula has set up small tables in a sunny spot, her microscope, and magnifying glasses for the kids to examine the bugs and plant life. Some of the cottagers collected water samples from three different areas of the lake this morning.

The children jostle to get a look. They are doing science, even if they don't know it. Their findings will be sent to scientists tracking the lake's water quality, curious to see how these samples compare to last year's results. Ursula loves it here. She can leave her cares and the city behind. Others should be able to enjoy it too, for many years to come. She is doing what she can to protect the water and the land in this lovely place.

Ursula became one of Canada's early environmentalists. An environmentalist is a person who works to protect the earth's water, air, minerals, creatures, and plants. When Ursula was growing up, most people thought that resources were unlimited.

> In the land that would become Canada, Indigenous peoples have taken care of nature for centuries. Over many generations, they studied their environment and understood they had an important role to play in using it in a way that was best for all species. It's important to understand this because it shows us that our current climate crisis is not the way it has always been. It is not the way it should be. And it is not the way it needs to be.

If they used something up in one area, they would just move to the next place. If all the trees were cut down in the forest or all the fish were caught in an ocean, people thought that nature just somehow repaired itself. They didn't think there was a problem if cities dumped their waste into the local lake. Most of them had no idea that human activities could permanently damage the environment, and that we needed to protect it.

For many years, governments and big companies understood their activities could destroy nature, but they thought that the destruction was worth the reward, so they didn't curb their harm. Ursula learned about some of these harmful activities through her research as a young university student, and through the radiation studies she did with VOW. So, just like she did whenever she noticed a public problem, Mom got involved. My father joined in too. In the '60s and '70s, I remember his taking part in early efforts to study the impact of mercury poisoning in Indigenous communities in northern Ontario. A company had been dumping highly poisonous chemicals into a river, and it caused a lot of illness and death in nearby communities, tearing families apart.

Being an environmentalist is not just about getting involved in big public campaigns. It's also about what you can do as an individual. You can help the environment by taking actions in your own life, even if they may seem small. My parents felt it was important to live very simply and frugally so that we wouldn't have a negative impact on our surroundings. Our whole family walked, used public transit, or rode bicycles to get where we needed to be.

Mother joined our local residents' association whose goal was to make sure that any new buildings constructed in the area fit in and became part of the neighborhood. They thought that new buildings should not tower over the homes and businesses that were already there. They wanted decisions affecting the neighborhood to have input from the people who lived and worked there; decisions based on what was best for the community.

Cottage life in Muskoka. The family spent many summers up here together.

Left to right: Monica's husband, Raul, their eldest son, Alejandro, Ursula, and Monica.

When I was growing up, we spent summers on a small lake in Muskoka. We lived very simply there too. Our small, rustic cabin didn't have hot water or even a telephone! Martin and I spent our summer days playing outside, swimming, and going up and down the lake in our small rowboat. Mom did much of her thinking, reading, and writing there. She was involved in the local community at the cottage too. She joined the lake association, which encouraged cottagers to limit their environmental impact on the lake. She and the other members tested the lake water for pollution and talked to their fellow cottagers about not using fertilizer on the grass,

Report from the Science Council of Canada, "Canada as a Conserver Society: Resource Uncertainties and the Need for New Technologies," 1977.

or soap and shampoo in the lake. Ursula wrote many letters to the local council about the environmental dangers of having too many people on such a small lake. It wasn't that Ursula was against growth or change. She simply felt they needed to happen in a way that respected the earth's environment and resources.

Over time, people came to realize that Canada's natural resources were *not* unlimited. And so, in the 1970s, Ursula was invited to lead a committee that would come up with a uniquely Canadian energy policy. It examined how people were using electricity and gas (for cars), where we were getting these resources from, and how these actions might need to change.

Ursula and her committee members researched all aspects of society, from housing and transportation to supplies of things such as electricity and fossil fuel. Their report was called "Canada as a Conserver Society: Resource Uncertainties and the Need for New Technologies." Their conclusion was that Canadian society needed to change. It needed to shift from a *consumer* society to a *conserver* society. A consumer society is where we use more and more goods and natural resources until the planet has nothing left. In a conserver society, we try to use less and take care of the resources we have. We try to find new sources of energy. The report said that our consumer society was damaging the environment. It also said that regular citizens should decide the best path for Canada moving forward.

The committee's ideas about consumer and conserver societies were almost unheard of at the time. And they were not very popular. Some thought they would mean that Canada couldn't be a wealthy country anymore. Others did not understand why they should have to make any urgent changes. It just didn't seem all that important. Ursula and her colleagues were disappointed. Once again, it seemed like all the work they had done was basically ignored. Now though, many people are praising the Conserver Society Report for being ahead of its time. They say that its findings and conclusions are more relevant now than ever.

Even though the report was ignored at the time, Ursula was not about to give up on protecting the environment. In 1996, she helped form a group called Citizens' Environmental Watch. She and the cofounders created this group because the government of Ontario had cut back funding dollars to spend on environmental issues. The group's goal was to involve people in their local natural surroundings. This meant they wouldn't have to rely on the government to act. Instead, regular citizens would take an active role to protect the land and water around them. We now call these people "citizen scientists." This term recognizes that even if you don't know a lot about science, you can still notice how the plants and animals are behaving around you and share that information with a scientist.

We often expect activist work to have a large, immediate impact on society—and that the change will last forever. But it usually isn't like that. When it comes to big issues, such as gaining equal rights for women, people of color, and LGBTQ+ individuals, or taking action on global warming, change can be very slow. It's easy to get discouraged when we work so hard for something but don't see the rewards right away. And maybe we're afraid that we will be ignored, or laughed at, or even harmed because we stand up for what we believe in. But we can't let anything discourage us from trying. Like Ursula, we have to keep going, because someday it *will* make a difference.

> Citizen's Environmental Watch was renamed EcoSpark in 2010. The group now focuses on getting kids involved in science. EcoSpark works with teachers and communities to design science projects that encourage young people to explore wildlife in their neighborhoods. On June 15, 2023, EcoSpark turned twenty-five years old, and there was a big party to celebrate.

# Chapter 12

# Ursula the Innovator

The classroom is full of students curious to learn about this new field, *archaeometry*. Ursula and Maxine, her colleague from the Department of Anthropology, stand at the lecture podium. They introduce the object for today's discussion: a fragment of pottery from Greece. Where did it come from? Who made it? What's it for? How old is it? Maxine talks first, and then it's Ursula's turn. She puts the piece under the microscope and points out what she sees on the projector screen at the front of the classroom. "Look at the cracks running through the piece of pottery. The edges look shiny, don't they?"

The students agree the fragment is probably an everyday item—maybe a water jug—with a design on it. Someone speaks up. "Is that dirt? A leaf?" This is interesting. They'll need to do more testing.

Ursula is already thinking of other objects she can bring when, just for a moment, she too, slips into the past. She sees her own small hands holding an ancient object in her parents' Berlin home. The memory makes her smile. She immediately decides what she will bring to the next class; that African figure she saw wrapped in cloth at the ROM. It has been there so long that the cloth has imprints from the figure on it. She knows it has a story to tell.

When Ursula first began to work full-time in the Faculty of Engineering, she had felt very alone. Being the only female in the department, she faced challenges and resentment from the male student body and from coworkers, many of whom didn't appreciate her strong stance against military funding. They needed that money for their research.

In her early days at U of T, Ursula met with a difficult and unfriendly workplace. So, she developed her own area of expertise, which helped her thrive in the department. Her field of study was metallurgy, or metals. She examined the chemicals that make up different types of metals and how they can be used to make many things, from jewelry to buildings to batteries. But Ursula became more and more interested in how objects that already existed were made—especially if they were made from metal. Once again, she wanted to know *who* made them, *how* and *why* they were made.

> We often think of objects from the past as being simpler than the high tech that many of us use in our daily lives. And so, because the objects are simpler, it should be easy to figure out where they came from and what people used them for. But in truth, when we discover historical artifacts, we don't always know much about their origins. Like us, people from the past used all kinds of tools to help them grow food, make clothes, create art, pray, learn, and celebrate the world around them. Maybe they developed the tools themselves, or maybe they got them from traders from other countries. People have always been creative and changed with the times, so a historical object can often seem strange to us! It can be hard to guess what it may have been used for.

Ursula had really enjoyed her time working with the ROM, where she used her technical skills to figure out the ages of ancient objects. There, she had realized that her techniques could also show *how* the objects were made. She could use a microscope or an X-ray to look at the very tiny details of things such as a piece of fabric, pottery, or an arrowhead. When you look at fabric under a microscope, you can see the threads. You can see whether the threads are thick or thin and figure out whether they

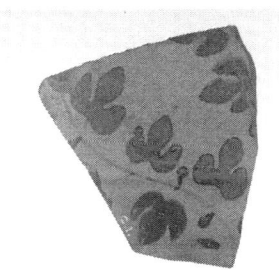
Caption tk.

Ursula the Innovator  73

are made from wool, horsehair, silk, linen, or cotton. You can see whether the threads are woven tightly, or whether they are loose. Then, you might be able to guess whether the fabric was made on a loom or by hand. You can also see small grains of dust from plant matter, food, makeup, dirt, or animal fur on the fabric. With more tests, these grains of information might be able to tell you where and when the fabric was made.

Ursula wanted to expand her work by creating a brand-new research area combining her skills with microscopes and X-rays and her interest in how objects were made. It was important to her that this research matched her values and beliefs. Whether she was protesting with the feminists, studying the impacts of radiation, or volunteering with the Quakers, Ursula's focus was on people. Not on wealthy or powerful people, but the ordinary people who had the most to gain, or lose, in any situation. That's who Ursula cared about.

"Studies in Ancient Peruvian Metalworking," published through the Royal Ontario Museum in 1979.

In the past, it was usually the common people who crafted and used the objects that we now study and admire in museums. It was often women who made them. To this day, many museums have large collections of objects that have gone unstudied *because* they were made and used by women and therefore deemed unimportant. Mother was one of the first scientists who tried to change this.

Ursula called her new scholarly field *archaeometry*. It was an area of work that was not of much interest to her colleagues in the Engineering Department, and it had nothing to do with the military. She could work independently and did not have to rely on her engineering colleagues. Instead, she found professors and researchers in other departments and from outside the university who shared her interest in learning about ancient objects and nondestructive techniques.

While she was creating this brand-new field of study, Ursula was still working as a professor. She decided to introduce archaeometry in a course for advanced students who were continuing their studies and doing further research. It was not just the subject matter that was unique: the way the course was taught was also unusual. Ursula co-taught the course with the head of the Department of Anthropology. Each class meeting was like a conversation between the two teachers. The anthropologist would talk about where an object came from and how it was used, and then Ursula would say what more they might learn by looking at the object under a microscope or by doing tests for chemicals and examining the small grains of dust that were left on it. The archaeometry classes were not only fascinating. They were popular for their strong spirit of cooperation.

Ursula knew there were others who were interested in this new field. She wanted to create a space where researchers could come together and share their knowledge and skills. So, she formed a group that brought together researchers from all different departments within universities and outside of them: engineering, history, art, archaeology, science, women's studies, and many others. She called the group the *Collegium Archaeometricum*.

In the Collegium, researchers supported each other and shared their findings. No one was in charge, and no one was beneath anyone else. It was just like the Quaker meetings. She wanted each person to feel that they were a valued member of the group. In fact, the word *collegium* means a group in which each member has equal power and authority. Everyone's ideas were important. If one person was stuck on a problem, they could discuss it with the group and find a solution together. And because they all had different research specialties, they all had something to teach to, and to learn from, their peers. Archaeometry became revolutionary in the way it

> The word *archaeometry* combines *archaeo*, which means ancient (like in *archaeology*), with *metry*, which relates to measuring things (like in *geometry*). Archaeometry is the study of ancient artifacts using modern science with modern methods. An important part of archaeometry is finding new ways to collect scientific evidence without harming the objects.

"Ursula at home in her office." Published in the *University of Toronto Magazine* summer 1989 issue, "Ages of Irrelevance: The Metallurgist as Archaeologist," written by Karina Dahlin.

connected archaeologists, materials scientists, and historians. It is now recognized as a distinct field, separate from archaeology. Ursula's Collegium continues to this day in the form of the international research journal *Archaeometry*.

All in all, Ursula spent twenty-two years at U of T. She was influential in her university department and faculty and in the wider community. She was an innovator in science and engineering. She supported, encouraged, and promoted others, especially women. From technology to peace and social justice, she wrote and spoke about issues that were important to her. For all her work, dedication, and determination, she received countless honors and awards.

But then, in September 1986, it all might have come to a halt. Ursula had reached sixty-five years of age, and the law in Ontario said she had to retire from work. But she wasn't ready to stop!

# Part V

A Different Kind of Senior Citizen

## Chapter 13

# Ursula the Retired Professor

Ursula looks out her Massey College window. The lawn in front is full of students talking, eating lunch on benches, rushing to classes. How lucky she is to have ended up at Massey College! Finally, she has time to think, reflect, and write—and a room to do it in. She's already planning to write a book about technology and its impact on society. She also wants to write about her profession. There are now more women in engineering, but are they truly equal? She wants to think more about Quakerism and the link between faith and action. Ursula smiles inwardly. She may be sixty-five, but she isn't finished yet. There's still so much to do.

    Ursula glances at the clock. It's almost noon. Her daughter, Monica, now a law student, is coming for lunch. Maybe she can introduce Monica to her neighbors here at Massey. Susan and Patrick are both judges. The three of them would have a lot to talk about. One of the best things about Massey, thinks Ursula, is connecting people who might otherwise never meet, or realize how much they have in common. It has always been one of her greatest pleasures, and now, she can share it with Monica!

Massey College is a special residence for graduate students at the University of Toronto. Only a small number of students live there, and they're all interested in different subjects. Some like science or history, and others like art, medicine, law, or languages. Usually, university students only socialize with people from their own departments, but at Massey College they all live together and get to share ideas and learn from each other. This is very unique! It is also very much in keeping with Ursula's dedication to collaboration.

When my mother turned sixty-five, she must have celebrated her birthday with mixed feelings. She had accomplished many things and had been very active throughout her career. But at that time in Canada, it was the law that everyone who was still working had to stop at age sixty-five. Ursula was allowed to keep her office in the Wallberg Building until the end of the month. After that, she would no longer be a professor at U of T. She had worked there for almost twenty years and now she had been set adrift! This was very hard on her. She had received so much recognition, so many awards—she had even been appointed the first woman university professor (the highest academic rank at the University of Toronto), in 1984. But after all her achievements, once she reached the age of retirement, it seemed like society viewed her as a senior citizen.

Back then, people thought that senior citizens couldn't work in the same way they had before—that their intellect wasn't as sharp, and their body couldn't keep up. Things aren't a whole lot different today. Although the laws have changed, many of us still tend to think that a person's value is based on their youth, how much work they can do, and how quickly they can do it. We sometimes ignore the priceless knowledge and experience that older people have gained. We don't always realize that they still aspire to achieve things. They still have hopes and dreams for the future as they age, and they still have a lot to contribute.

My mother must have felt cast aside. As I think about it now, she may have felt much the same as when she first came to Canada; as if her entire past was gone and everything ahead was foreign to her. But being a proactive person, Mom wasn't about to sit on the sidelines for long.

First, Ursula was offered the position of Director of the Museum Studies Program at U of T. Having a lifelong fascination for ancient objects, Ursula was interested. As director, she could encourage students and professors from different areas of research to work together and share their knowledge. This was similar to what she had done at the Collegium Archaeometricum. She could also help students obtain internships at museums and galleries where they would learn more about the history and purpose of ancient objects.

Ursula accepted the position and stayed for two years. But she was not destined to remain there. Our whole family wondered what Mom would do next. I could not imagine her working from home. To begin with, there wasn't room for her there. My father, Fred, had been a full-time volunteer and activist in his own right for many years. He worked with the Quakers, particularly on human rights and social justice issues. He also ran a Quaker program in the Toronto jails and immigration detention centers. He wanted to ensure that incarcerated people knew they had not been forgotten and that they still mattered. The program connected inmates to help and services. Sometimes it was a book club: everyone would read a book and discuss it at the next meeting. The group might talk about everyone's different traditions, such as for birthdays or New Years. At other times, they might talk about what university or college courses they wanted to take. They often talked about violence and better ways of resolving conflicts. Or about world events or their families. The program was really about breaking down the barriers between people in detention and those "on the outside."

Fred was certainly busy! All the tables, countertops, beds, and even the ironing board were covered in his papers. Ursula really needed to have her own place to work. Somewhere where she would feel valued and appreciated. That turned out to be Massey College.

Ursula joined Massey College as a Senior Fellow in 1989. Her role was to talk about her interests and research with the students and to help them in their studies. If the students did not know already, they quickly found out about Ursula's activism. She mentored the female students, showing them how someone can succeed in a male-dominated profession and how it's possible to connect research and academic life with social justice.

Massey College did present some challenges to Ursula though. When the College was set up in 1962, women were not allowed. It took until 1974 for that to change. When Ursula first came to Massey, some of the male professors didn't like that she was there. One even refused to speak to her! Sometimes she did not agree when the college proposed that certain professors become Senior Fellows, and she said so. But overall, Ursula was very happy there. Whenever she arrived at her office in the morning, she would find students and faculty waiting to speak to her. Mother often brought guests—including my father, brother, and me—to Massey for lunch. She enjoyed the food, but the company, and the conversation were what she really loved.

Ursula did a lot of writing and deep thinking while she was at Massey. Much of her time was filled with public speaking engagements. She was often asked to write things for magazines, newspapers, and books and to speak on the radio. In 1989, she recorded a lecture series on CBC Radio that she called *The Real World of Technology*. It was about how technology is more than wheels, gears, and electronics. It is a whole system that affects everything in people's lives.

Think about how much we use the internet to communicate and find information today. Compare it to earlier ways—letters, telephone calls, and libraries. The internet alone has completely changed how and what we share with others and how fast we can do it. And there are so many other technologies coming along every day! Sometimes they bring changes that are beneficial. Sometimes the changes are harmful, and sometimes they are both. Ursula said that technology is not something neutral. It reflects the people who design it as well as those who use it. That's what Ursula explored in her lectures. Three years later, the lectures were published as a book. People considered it so important that they asked Ursula to write more on the topic. An expanded version of the book was published in 1999. In 2021, CBC Radio even reran the lectures. What Ursula said in 1989 was still very relevant thirty-two years later.

Originally recorded in 1989, Ursula's CBC Massey Lectures are available online in both audio and print formats.

◆

On December 6, 1989, a terrible thing happened in Montreal. A man who had failed to qualify for École Polytechnique de Montréal (now called Polytechnique Montréal), killed fourteen engineering students—all of them women. He blamed them for taking the spot he thought belonged to him. The event became known as the Montreal Massacre, and it deeply affected Ursula. She knew, as our whole family did, that if this man had been in Toronto rather than Montreal, she would have been at the top of his list of people to target, and her students would have been the ones killed.

Ursula spoke at the University of Toronto's memorial event the following month. Her words were considered both brave and controversial. She said it was easy to overlook the massacre as the one-time action of a madman. Instead, she urged people to consider how much violence occurs against women in male-dominated fields. Ursula pointed out that the gunman had told the men to leave the room before he began shooting. Ursula asked people to think about what true equality and solidarity mean. In this case, it should have meant that the women belonged at the school because they had earned their places, just like the male students. All the students, both male and female, had a role to play in making the classroom a fair and equitable place. A threat against the women students should have been seen as a threat against *all* engineering students.

> Tax refusers are people who, because of their religious beliefs, will not contribute money to be spent on war, weapons, or the military. They recognize the need and support paying for social programs, schools, roads, etc. They just do not want their money used for violence. The problem is that it is against the law to not pay *all* of your taxes.

Ursula's address was published in a special issue of a journal called *Canadian Women's Studies* and was also read into the record of the Canadian Senate on February 21, 1990. Whether readers agreed with her or not, Ursula stood her ground and gave people much to think about.

While at Massey, Mother continued to write about Quakerism and how faith can, and should, influence the actions people take in their daily lives. And true to her faith, Mom took an active role in the things that mattered to her. One of them was the legal case of Dr. Jerilynn Prior, also a Quaker and scientist. She refused to pay a portion of her taxes because she knew that some of it would go toward supporting the military. This made Prior a tax refuser.

The government tax office insisted that Prior pay her total tax amount, so she decided to take the matter to court. She argued that her decision to withhold some tax dollars was based on her freedom of conscience and freedom of religion. Those are both guaranteed freedoms under the Canadian Charter of Rights and Freedoms. Ursula worked with Prior's lawyer to gather information explaining the Quaker religion (and particularly the basis for its opposition to war dating back to the 1600s) to the court. Unfortunately, Prior lost her case. Even so, Ursula felt that they had achieved something. Ursula, Prior, and the lawyer had put together a valid legal argument about actions taken based on pacifist beliefs. This meant that future lawyers could look at the case, learn from it, and try to figure out how such a case could be successful one day.

Ursula said their work was preparing the soil, like earthworms do. She said that earthworms teach us that soil needs to be prepared before anything grows. It is the same for creative thinking and ways of resolving problems—the world needs to be prepared and open to new ideas before they can flourish. Ursula felt that the arguments made in support of Prior's position may not have convinced the judges, but hopefully they paved the way for a time when minds were more open. That was good enough for Ursula. As always, she was looking to the future and working to make society better and fairer for following generations.

# Chapter 14

# Ursula the Academy

Ursula stands on a podium with the Chair of the Toronto School Board, some trustees, the school principal, staff, and a few parents. The first class of grade nine students sits before her, eager and excited. This is the opening of the Ursula Franklin Academy (UFA).

Ursula takes a moment to really study the young people gathered here. Not too long from now, in June 2000, she expects to see them come together again to celebrate the school's first graduating class. The students will have matured slightly, but if she sees the same expressions of hope and eagerness on their faces, she'll know "her school" has fulfilled its mission. These young people will be well prepared and confident to take their next steps into a bigger community.

She tells them that she wants UFA to be an exciting place of learning, a place for building lasting friendships among students, parents, and teachers. Not only will they take their education and friendships with them, but her greatest hope is that their hunger for lifelong learning and positive action will be ignited.

My mother worked hard throughout her career. She stood for things that were important to her. She didn't worry about being "the first woman" or "the only one" to think in a certain way. She had faced resistance, harassment, and discrimination. But now, she was finally being recognized. She received awards and honorary degrees from universities across Canada. Universities present honorary degrees to recognize all the achievements someone has accomplished. And Ursula had accomplished a lot. She had also become a Member of the Order of Canada (the highest award in Canada), and a recipient of a Governor General's Award and the Pearson Peace Medal. But then along came a new and different honor: a brand-new school named after her.

Ursula had been passionate about teaching ever since she was back in Germany, where she helped junior students with their research. As a professor at U of T, and later at Massey College, she taught and mentored hundreds of students. Supporting the next generation of scholars was her way of furthering knowledge that would last well into the future. My mother wanted that to be her legacy.

Education and school were also personal for her. She had been a student before she was a teacher, so she understood the exciting challenges and difficult struggles. Plus, she had seen my brother and me navigate the public school system in Toronto. Now she watched our children, her four grandchildren, doing the same.

School can be tough, and students don't always get the support or opportunities they need. I had been frustrated in my downtown Toronto high school in the 1970s. I found it too large and impersonal. The staff did not seem very interested in me as a learner. I wanted to study things that were not in the courses and wanted more depth. I left that high school after three years to go to an alternative school called SEED. Alternative schools usually have smaller class sizes and use experimental or hands-on teaching styles. They give students more of a say in what they learn and how they learn it.

Martin liked the same high school that I hated, and he navigated it better than I did. He had difficulties later when he left to go to university. It was his first time living away from home and he wasn't sure about what he was studying. He ended up dropping out. He returned to university many years later and became an elementary school teacher.

In the early 1990s, Ursula was approached by a group of trustees, educators, and parents who had been working on setting up a new kind of public high school. They wanted a school that focused on languages, math, science, and technology, with a curriculum that would prepare its students for the modern digital world.

Sketch of the Ursula Franklin Academy in Toronto, by Katherine Khasimkhana, 2019.

Mother was intrigued! The more she thought about it, the more she liked the concept. It was an opportunity to combine the arts with sciences and to use technology in a way that supported the students. The planning group then looked for a worthy namesake for the school. They approached Ursula again, this time to ask if they could name the school after her.

Initially, Ursula wasn't sure. She felt a school in her name put too much attention on her. Ursula resisted the idea for quite a long time, but in the end, she agreed. Why? Because the planning committee promised that Ursula could be actively involved in setting up the school—what and how it taught—and that she could be as involved as she liked in all aspects of the program. She was finally persuaded that this school, with her name on it, would truly reflect what she believed in and stood for.

At that time, schools were named after people who had died to remember and honor them. Ursula Franklin Academy was the first school named after someone who was still living. And it was the only school in the Toronto Board of Education that was named solely after a woman. Mom, without intending to, was still accomplishing meaningful "firsts!"

Ursula was very committed to the public school system because she liked how it brought families from different backgrounds together. She wanted it to be truly public—not a private or independent school (where parents had to pay) or an alternative school or magnet school (with specialized courses). She wanted it to be safe and inclusive. She envisioned a school with students from all over Toronto to reflect the city's multicultural makeup and various economic backgrounds.

Ursula attended meetings with the planning committee and met regularly with the first school principal, Myrna Mathers. They helped ensure UFA students would flourish in a welcoming, challenging, and supportive environment. They decided that the school would be small, with only five hundred students, so that it would have a sense of community. Students would call teachers and staff by their first names so no one was perceived as better or "above" anyone else. This reflected Mother's Quaker beliefs. Quakers use first names to show that they value and respect each person, regardless of their job, wealth, or background.

It was important to Ursula that UFA students were involved in the world around them. Students would volunteer in their communities long before other public schools made it a graduation requirement. UFA would also offer minicourses based on students' interests: this was known as the Wednesday Enrichment Program. The minicourses would be open to all grades so students of different ages could interact. This was another way of breaking down high-school hierarchies.

Mom even chose the school colors! She selected navy blue, hunter green, and burgundy because they are not used on any country's national flag. Even when it came to colors, Mom didn't want to appear to support any country or culture over another.

Paper program from the first Ceremonial Opening at Ursula Franklin Academy, October 24, 1995.

> *Message from*
> **Dr. URSULA FRANKLIN**
>
> "Here are the three wishes that I have for the new academy:
>
> First of all, I hope that the school will be an exciting place of learning, where students will discover the joys and challenges of gaining knowledge and understanding.
>
> Then, I hope that the school will become a place for building lasting friendships among students, parents and teachers.
>
> And, finally, I hope that the endeavours being made in the school to build knowledge and understanding will extend out into the broader community and that the community, in turn, will enrich and support the goals and dreams of the school."

Excerpt from Ursula's speech at the Ceremonial Opening of Ursula Franklin Academy.

Ursula Franklin Academy opened in September 1995. It started with just grade nine students. As the grade nines moved up, new classes were added, one year at a time. Ursula attended events at "her school" and always tried to be available to UFA staff and students until her health slowed her down. She was delighted when my brother's sons, Nicholas and Andre, chose to attend Ursula Franklin Academy. To this day, UFA is known for being an innovative and vibrant Toronto public high school and is ranked among the best in the province of Ontario.

## Chapter 15

# Ursula the Plaintiff

Ursula walks up St. George Street to the courthouse. She is anxious and apprehensive. How did it come to this—taking the university to court? It's such a big step. She spent so many years at U of T and was always a good and loyal employee. As she walks, something catches her eye. Banners hang from the lampposts that line the street. They're for the university's big fundraising campaign. The banners bear the names and photos of important faculty. Ursula stops with a jolt. Staring back at her from a banner is her face. She almost laughs. The university thinks she is good enough to help them raise donations but not good enough to pay her properly!

Even though Ursula was retired, she was as busy as ever, writing, speaking, and enjoying the students at Massey College. To the people around her, it seemed like she had accomplished more than enough for one lifetime. But as always seemed to happen, a new challenge soon came her way.

The issue of pay inequity had followed Ursula through her life. Pay inequity is when people are paid different amounts of money even though they do the same job. This connects to the problems of the gender pay gap and the racial pay gap, where women and people of color are paid less for doing the same jobs as white men. These are issues that we continue to face to this day, as very often women and people of color are still not paid equally.

Ursula was pretty sure she had never been paid the same as the men around her, but it was hard to prove. When she was starting out as a young professor, people (and especially women) did not talk about money, or how much they were earning. Women felt lucky to have a job at all. Most were afraid to complain about their salaries because they didn't want to be fired. For Ursula, equal pay was a matter of principle: for women to be treated fairly, they had to be paid what men in the same job were making.

Women employees at the University of Toronto had been talking about pay inequity for years. There had been countless studies, salary reviews, and reports, including a big one in 1989. Because of that report, the university had to spend more than $800,000 to give women employees a one-time payout in 1991. But what about the women who were excluded from this payout? Some, like Ursula, had retired *before* 1991. They had dedicated decades of their lives to the university while receiving less money than they should have. Many of them were now living in poverty because their pensions were so low. The university refused to even talk about this group. They said they had already spent a lot of money on the 1991 payout and women who had retired before then were just out of luck.

What could be done? Some of these women knew each other. They had worked at the university at a time when female professors and staff were unusual. They had worked together on committees or projects or had met over common concerns. They had dealt with harassment and discrimination from male peers and students for years. Ursula and these women talked to each other for a long time, trying to find a solution. They wrote letters to the newspapers, to officials at U of T, including the president. The university wouldn't budge. They refused to meet with the women and didn't want to deal with the problem.

The women realized they had only one option left: to take the matter to court. They wanted to argue that the university discriminated against them by paying them less than men for decades. Studies showed that on average, women received only eighty cents for every dollar their male colleagues earned. For women of color, it was less than that.

This group of women wanted the university to compensate them for the missing twenty cents for every eighty cents they had earned during their time at the university. They would ask for their pensions to be adjusted too, since their pensions were calculated on what they had been paid, not on what they *should* have been paid.

A lawyer named Mary Eberts took the case. She decided to make it a class action, which meant a few specific people represented the whole group of people affected. In this case, all the women faculty who had retired before 1991. Ursula was asked to be one the women named in the case. At first, she was reluctant. She was eighty years old and had never been keen to put herself in the spotlight. She also didn't like the idea of going to court. In court cases, one side winning meant the other side lost. She preferred solutions where both sides could win.

But the more my mother thought about it, the more she felt she had a responsibility to the retired women. And she knew she was in a good position to speak out since she was retired and "famous." So, she agreed to join the other three plaintiffs: Blanche van Ginkel (the former Dean of Architecture), Cecily Watson (a founding professor of the Ontario Institute for Studies in Education), and Phyllis Grosskurth (the first woman professor in the Department of English).

Before the case could go to court, the four colleagues had to try to contact the many other women who'd retired before 1991. They also had to gather evidence. They needed specific information about the salary differences between men and women who did the same job. The university had data about salaries but not about the individuals themselves, who they were, and what jobs they performed. Thanks to a network of women and other interested people across the country, the needed data was gathered. The network reminded Ursula of how she had done the baby teeth study with Voice of Women in the 1960s.

It took over a year to gather all the information together. Finally, the case went to the Superior Court of Justice in September 2001. Ursula found the whole thing

From the *Toronto Star*, issue September 21, 2001. "Pension Issue: Ursula Franklin and Blanche van Ginkel, in the foreground left and right, hope to see their lawsuit against the University of Toronto certified as a class action, allowing them to represent 108 women, all former professors and librarians, who retired before the 1989 salary review settlement. Some 30 supporters showed up to back them yesterday in a Toronto courtroom."

Ursula and Blanche van Ginkel are surrounded by supporters and friends. In the crowd is also one of the witnesses in the case, Helen Breslauer. Today, this photo hangs in the Ursula Franklin Pay Equity Reading Room on the University of Toronto campus, which was officially opened on March 8, 2017.

incredibly stressful. She had been involved in all aspects of the case: creating the network and contributing information to it, drafting and redrafting documents, attending meetings with the lawyer, and dealing with countless emails. And now she had to go to court and give evidence to the judge.

Ursula was uncomfortable about that. The university had been her home and sanctuary for many years, and she had been loyal and committed to it in return. Through thick and thin, her work had gained respect, and she had friends and colleagues there. Still, the university had betrayed her, and she felt a responsibility to herself and others to gain equality. Ursula was hurt by some of the university president's comments and his unwillingness to try to settle the case out of court. In his previous job at a big American university, he had been quite supportive of women faculty, so this was a surprising disappointment. Was Ursula turning her back on all that she had worked for? No. Upsetting as it was, it was about her career and those of the women like her who had helped build the university. After all they had accomplished over the years, the school still refused to offer them equal pay and pensions. Ursula simply had to stand up and speak out.

In the beginning, there was not much interest about the case at U of T. Many people thought the issue was dead—they believed the 1991 payout had fixed all the pay inequalities between men and women. But the court proceedings were happening at the same time as the start of a big fundraising drive. The university was hoping to raise a billion dollars in donations from major corporations. People began to fear that the case would embarrass the university and make important funders reluctant to donate. The lawyers for the women and the university tried one last time to find a solution without having to go to court, but no one could agree on anything.

In the end, Judge Gans dismissed the case. The judge did not believe the case met the legal requirements to be considered a class action. He felt the four named women could not represent the whole group of female faculty who had retired before 1991. But it's important that he did not base his decision on the *evidence* they provided about the discrimination. In fact, the judge said he believed the women had strong arguments to sue the university individually. He thought that each of them should sue for compensation alone, instead of as a group. The judge encouraged the university to settle the matter without individual trials. If they didn't, they could face dozens of lawsuits. The university wisely decided to pay the women.

This meant that the legal world was ready to acknowledge that pay inequity was a real issue. It was a good outcome. Even though the four plaintiffs did not "win" their court case, the judge had heard and understood their position. Now, the financial settlement would reach more women and get money to them faster. This was important, since so many of them were in their eighties and nineties.

As a result of the case, about sixty retired women faculty received enhanced benefits. This meant a boost in their pensions. The university also put out a public statement saying that they recognized many female faculty had faced obstacles and barriers in their careers because of sexism. The public statement was important to Ursula because it showed that the university recognized its past injustices.

Ursula had come a long way from being "the only woman" harassed by the men around her, to finding respect and finally, to gaining the pension she had always deserved. Once again, my mother proved that it is possible to change things by standing up and working with others toward a common goal.

# Afterword

Mother was active well into her nineties! It was then that she could really reflect on her career and all she had accomplished. She had created a new area of study with archaeometry and had pioneered nondestructive ways to examine ancient artifacts. She had supported women both in university and outside of it. She had tirelessly advocated for peace, equality, and justice.

Through all of this, she had seen a lot of changes. Some things had changed for the better. Mom was delighted to hear the accounts of her oldest grandchild, my son Alejandro, when he enrolled in Engineering at the University of Toronto. The Dean of Engineering was a woman and a good percentage of the students were women. Alejandro was even studying in the same department (Materials Science) where Ursula had taught for almost twenty years! Change had not come fast enough in other areas though, so Ursula continued to write and speak out, ever curious and interested in the world around her.

Mother began to think about how her work and experiences could be preserved, so that others could benefit from them. She wanted people to know how things were for her and others like her because it's hard for young people today to imagine the challenges and discrimination women faced not so very long ago. Can *you* imagine a school building that had only one women's washroom but many for men? Or public university buildings where women were not even allowed? These things were real obstacles for Ursula, and she felt they should be recorded. Otherwise people might forget.

Some of the same challenges that my mother faced continue today and other new ones have surfaced. Life

A standing plaque, placed by the Toronto Legacy Project, outside of Ursula Franklin's former home in Toronto.

brings challenges, but when we forget about them or erase them from history, we lose the chance to see how people before us found a path forward. This is why Ursula believed it was important to leave records. Remembering the obstacles of the past is a way to make sure that no one will have to live through them again. Commemorating events such as the Montreal Massacre does the same thing. Every year on December 6, we remember the students who were murdered and reflect on violence against women. Looking back on how far we've come also helps us to remain positive. Mother wanted people to know that there is a way to overcome life's obstacles. Her path may have been different from the one someone might take today when facing similar challenges. The times are different. The important thing is to find a way to face problems head-on, like she did.

Mom gave her important records to the University of Toronto Archives. Archives are historical materials and documents that are housed in a library or a similar type of building. Ursula insisted that her archives collection be as complete as possible. It includes minutes from meetings (such as staff meetings, Science Council, and VOW meetings), course outlines, agendas, papers, personal letters and journals, interviews and recordings, newspaper articles and photos—more than a hundred and fifty boxes. It even includes her RCMP file!

Monica and Martin outside of the Ursula Franklin Pay Equity Reading Room at the University of Toronto.

Ursula Martius Franklin died on July 22, 2016, at the age of ninety-four, less than two months before her ninety-fifth birthday. She had repeatedly told us she did not want a big fuss. Nevertheless, the University of Toronto sent an email to all students and lowered the Canadian flag on the main campus. We held three memorial ceremonies: one at U of T (at Massey College), another at Ursula Franklin Academy, and a third at the Quaker meeting house in Toronto. Three memorials reflecting three different aspects of her life and activism. There were obituaries and testimonials from across Canada and the world. Many people spoke about her work and ideas and how important she had been to them.

Ursula lived courageously, according to her convictions, and she did what she knew was right. My mother was also always good company—a keen observer with a wicked sense of humor. She was devasted when my father showed signs of dementia late in his life. Fred had been her partner, companion, and sounding board for more than fifty years. He died six weeks after she did.

One of the things I miss most about my mother is her optimism. She was always looking to the future. She would be proud to know that what she built has outlived her. That people remember the things she said and did and still find them important and relevant. But she would be the first to say there is still so much to do! By working together, we can build a society that is fair, peaceful, and equitable for everyone. That's what my remarkable mother taught Martin, me, and so many others. That is her legacy.

My mother and I.

# Acknowledgments

Thank you to Myra N., who started the ball rolling and to my family for their support and encouragement. I'm so glad that my sons were able to know their extraordinary grandmother.

My thanks to my coauthor Erin as well as to editor Kathryn and all the folks at SSP for helping me tell my mother's story to a whole new generation.

—MF

I want to give a huge thank-you to Monica for inviting me to embark on this writing journey with her. Thank you for trusting me to help tell your mother's story. Thank you for your honesty, wisdom, and sense of conviction through this process, and thank you also for keeping me on track whenever I became too "speculative."

Thank you to Gillian Rodgerson for believing in me and for vouching for my abilities.

Major thanks to everyone at Second Story Press: Margie, Phuong, Emma, Michaela, and Kate. I appreciate all the work you do, not just in supporting this book but in supporting feminist publishing in Canada.

A massive thank-you to Jordan Ryder for her commitment to helping us see this project through.

Thank you to Hannah McAvoy for creating such an awesome book cover. Thank you to the book designer, Laura Atherton, for making this book look so good. And thank you to April Masongsong for ensuring that all the *t*s are crossed and *i*s are dotted.

So much gratitude for editor extraordinaire, Kathryn Cole. Thank you for taking such care with the manuscript and for guiding us through the revisions. You brought so much refinement to the prose, and this book would not have been the same without you.

And lastly, thank you to Ursula for preparing the soil.

—EDM

# Photo Credits

All photos are from the author's own collection unless stated below.

Pages 4 and 33 - Shutterstock
Pages 7, 12, 34, and 55 - University of Toronto Archives
Page 15 - The United States Holocaust Memorial Museum
Pages 28 and 29 - City of Toronto Archives
Page 50 - Library of Congress
Page 51 - Library and Collections Canada
Page 73 - Courtesy of ROM (Royal Ontario Museum), Toronto, Canada. ©ROM
Page 76 - Michael Wallace
Page 93 - Tannis Toohey

# About the Authors

**Monica Franklin** grew up in an unusual family in 1960s Toronto. She came to realize how unique her mother, Ursula Franklin, was: a Holocaust survivor, a professor in Engineering at the University of Toronto, a feminist, pacifist, educator, and environmentalist. Monica is a retired lawyer living in Toronto with her family. She is very pleased that her children were able to know, enjoy, and learn from their maternal grandmother, Ursula Franklin.

**Erin Della Mattia** is a writer and editor from Brampton, Ontario. Her fiction has appeared in *The Puritan* and in the fairy tale anthology *Sharper Than Thorns*. Although her collection of book ideas grows ever larger, she can usually be found elbow-deep in the brilliant mire of someone else's manuscript.